Nostradamus

Hidden Messages Revealed for the First Time

(Forecasting Tomorrow Today by the Lens of Technologies)

Daniel Witt

Published By **Oliver Leish**

Daniel Witt

Nostradamus: Hidden Messages Revealed for the First Time (Forecasting Tomorrow Today by the Lens of Technologies)

ISBN 978-1-990373-81-7

No part of this guidebook shall be reproduced in any form without permission in writing from the publisher except in the case of brief quotations embodied in critical articles or reviews.

Legal & Disclaimer

The information contained in this book is not designed to replace or take the place of any form of medicine or professional medical advice. The information in this book has been provided for educational & entertainment purposes only.

The information contained in this book has been compiled from sources deemed reliable, and it is accurate to the best of the Author's knowledge; however, the Author cannot guarantee its accuracy and validity and cannot be held liable for any errors or omissions. Changes are periodically made to this book. You must consult your doctor or get professional medical advice before using any of the suggested remedies, techniques, or information in this book.

Table Of Contents

Chapter 1: Language Of Starry Sky Astrology.. 1

Chapter 2: Astrogeography And Our Country 30

Chapter 3: Planet Parade - The Mystery Of Our Time 55

Chapter 4: The Soviet Union At The Crossroad Of Epoch............................... 84

Chapter 5: The World Of The Future 126

Chapter 6: Life And Times Of The Prophet 154

Chapter 1: Language Of Starry Sky Astrology

The oldest science and art of the divine, offering an all-encompassing view of the world as well as one of the types of understanding the world. ' It is a method of information about the future. It is indissociably linked to the past and present. They all blend in a single, unifying process of ETERNITY. So, the happenings of the future distant are simple to predict. Astrology doesn't provide precise predictions but it does provide a projection of the most likely time. The Astrologer P. Globa predicted the death of V. Vysotsky, the blast at the Chernobyl nuclear power station, the earthquakes that struck Armenia and Tajikistan and the fall of the Warsaw Pact, the democratic revolutions that took place in Eastern Europe, and the loss of N. Ceausescu.

In spite of the certain certainty of things and programmable human fates individuals are increasingly aware of their own actions and free-will, thereby avoiding chances to an irreversible stone (fatum) because of which one can alter his own behavior and conduct in the most unlikely, crucial scenario. The early Greek scientist Claudius Ptolemy (90-160 AD) declared: "The stars incline, but do not oblige." The freedom of will of a individual is a strange interaction with the blind destiny, which in the beginning determines the destiny of the person as well as the order of events that occur in his life. In order to determine how the horoscope for the next year is constructed.

The HOROSCOPE drawing is geometric depicting the locations of the planets as well as the Moon as well as the Sun in the sky of stars with respect to the horizon at the birthplace (or the conception) of an individual (organization or condition, or organization).

It is a holy circle (mandala) that contains geo-metric symbols are engraved by taking into consideration the location of the celestial bodies and this allows you to understand some laws that are beyond our comprehension of the universe. It is a fact that birthing into this world and emerging from the mother's womb and a father, from the very initial moment of birth, a person is struck by the powerful impact of the stars' radiation and, as it happens is able to inscribe into him a codes that are formed.

Its further growth - mental and physical.

Mandal lets you judge the most crucial and fatal moments in human existence, and which point in his life one is required to be extremely cautious and careful when making decisions. It aids in understanding the traits that characterize the person's capabilities and tendencies and the direction for the most effective self-improvement potential life challenges and their time of appearance. The study of a birth horoscope helps us determine if a person is in healthy health, which ailments and times he could be afflicted, what to do best to manage him, and when of the each day it is best to seek medical attention. You can for each individual create 12 horoscopes because the person is multidimensional and manifests in various states, worlds and states in various ways. Apart from the horoscope that reflects the life-span of a person can also be made the cosmogram of personality which is an karmic plan, which reflects the ultimate potential of an individual from the viewpoint that of the Cosmos. Actually, the horoscope is the actual manifestation of karma within certain terrestrial environments.

The purpose of astrology is to predict the future. It's a type of advisor, that helps create a defence mechanism for the human body that protects the body from negative results, as well as boost confidence in self. Understanding the plan of the human life must be utilized to improve self-confidence as well as a complication to the evolution pathway. It is true that people born under the signs of Cancer, Capricorn, Vodeleya and Pisces can benefit from interpret astrology. The future of us isn't at first set in stone, it's multivariate and anyone or the entire human race is able to modify his life, to transform the way within which they live as a human being has the energy of God and a light of divine light that creates the world a different place and uncertain. The universe is governed by a set of laws and astrology permits people to understand their reason for being. It can prepare one for a place in the systems of information, and the search for information that is embedded within its structure.

The Middle Ages, great astrologers were in the fatalism position - the inevitable, the immutability of rock, fatum.

Then there was Nostradamus (1503-1566) was a prophet who predicted the future in 2242 (from 1555 to 3797 which is which is the Year of the end of the World or the 797th year of the biblical Creation of the World in 4757 BC) as well as the likelihood of confirmation at 95 per cent. He was an unquestionable mortalist. He was largely disaffected from the traditional spiritual doctrines that provided man with a chance to grow and transform qualitatively as well as participation in the destiny of his life and in the fates of the universe as individuals are part of Cosmos. Nostradamus was a man made of the Fatum toy in the belief that nothing could alter his destiny, which is his fate is determined through the his horoscope.

The prophet Nostradamus foretold the outcome of Napoleon I:

1794 1st of July, 1794 "A courageous warrior was born in Italy.

The Empire will soon be the midst of a rebellion! How many soldiers have the soldiers you killed. Fantastic butcher in an unwinnable war! The simple soldier can sit in the throne of French rulers and take on all of Europe by winning a battle. His boots are able to cross the borders of Europe's eastern side. He will then go back to the island and die in the sand islands. "

Around the time of the XX century the soothsayer who was clever said in a qutrain that was encrypted (quatrain):

"The twentieth century is brutal and horrible,

The two wars of the century, dictatorship of slaves, and science with a bloody flame because of a lack of faith, God will make gods. "

M. Nostradamus also predicted the siege of the Turks of Vienna (1520) as well as the discovery made by The Portuguese of Japan (1546) and the discovery made by those who were French of Canada (1535) and the St. Bartholomew night (1572) as well as the subsequent maintenance of the Gregorian calendar (1597) and the principles from G. Galileo (1606) as well as the creation of the thermometer (1618) The 30-year "war to preserve to preserve the Spanish inheritors' (1618-1648), the discovery of the British

Australia (16-12) The time of Louis XIV (1643-1715), the the steam engine and Polzunov (1763) The Independence of the United States (1776), the balloon's creation (1773) as well as the French Revolution (1789), the invention of electricity (1795) and the fall of Napoleon I in Russia and the fire that destroyed Moscow (1812) The creation of the railway (1825) and the development of the telephone (1844) The development of a new philosophical system that was Marxism-Engelsism (1848-1859) and the Austro-Italian Wars

(1848-1849, 1866) The invention of the dynamite (1867) as well as the development of the Suez Canal (1869), the development of the lamp (1873) as well as a telephone (1876) as well as the opening of the beams of Xrays (1895) and the conclusion of the Aiglo-Boer war (1902) and the development of the first aircraft by the brothers. Wright (1903) The development the use of chemicals (1907) as well as The Balkan Wars (1912-1913), the establishment of the Panama Canal (1914), the assassination of the Austrian king. Austrian

Archduke Franz Ferdinand, which gave birth to World War I (1914) and the October Revolution in Russia (1917) and the debut of the television (1925) as well as the voyage of C. Lindberg across the Atlantic Ocean (1927), the first sound film (1927) The Great Economic Depression

(1929-1933) (1929-1933) social democrats, and Hitler became the rulers of Germany by greeting the German people (1933) The Spanish Civil War (1936-1939). at the start of the Second World Warriors (19:59) The creation of the nuclear bomb (1945) and the initial flight of Chelopsk to space (1961) The first American moonwalk Moon (1969). The fascist party said:

"Grand myths will deceive people, II will commit many evils. Power in its malice will suffocate, The state of beasts does not live a long age. "

The prophet also predicted the appearance of intelligent aliens in space during the 20th century, as well as weather disturbances due to frequent rocket launches as well as floods, and the emergence of new diseases (AIDS) as well as the discovery of a treatment for cancer (19902e) which was the replacement of the black (coal) energy by the white (atomic). The brilliant "dreamer foresaw not only the technical discoveries of our co. 'S - submarines, airplanes, the hydrogen" the yum. However, there was also 4E-1enie that is on the ground! Some of them include General de Gaulle, Franco, Lenin, " Stalin, Hitler, Mussolini.

A great astrologer R. Nehru (15th century) utilized a different method for predicting his "Oracle." The belief was that it is up to mankind's ability to decide to take a different route for his progress. Unfortunately, the human race has not yet escaped from the cycle of destruction. What is the point of knowing his destiny if it's unavoidable? We are merely puppets, toys that are in the hands Fate and there is no reason to try and fight it? No, not really. If we know our own future every one of us is able to figure out the best way to fulfill our potential and our purpose to Earth. Individuals can correct, alter their destiny, their time. In the end, the changes in the historical wheel largely depend on the governing bodies of countries. Astrology warns us about possibility of a life full of turbulences which prompts people to make the best decision in order to avoid a disastrously miserable situation. This is when the battle with Good and Evil within our lives becomes tension-filled. Based on the individual's horoscope, we is able to determine the forces that the person will join based on the choices he's made during this time. The universe is multi-dimensional. and at every moment, the individual is a multidimensional being in general there's no one the way, as well as the three alternatives, i.e., the Horoscope provides options for certain times. Life is apparently affected by two elements that are at work: one the path is dictated by the patterns that are that are reflected in the horoscope at birth, and on the other hand, it is determined by the individual involvement of the individual.

The central tenet of old Iranian philosophical-astrological astrologer "Avesta" (6th century before and. E.) It is an alteration in man his own internal process improvement in self. Avestan astrology, closely connected to the religious and moral doctrine of Zarathustra it is based upon observations which lasted for longer than 26000 years. The principle that drives it is the insanity that the Universe has. The same thing that happens to similar components, or particles in the Universe is what will happen with the same circumstances with other elements in the unbreakable universe. The principle behind holography is that each part replicates the entire.

The sky with stars provides the ideal micro model to understand how the heavenly laws. They are primarily manifested through the motion of the planets. This can be measured both from the past as well as in the near future. Concentrating on the locations of celestial bodies it is possible to conclude that there are actions that occur on Earth as the movement of the Sun as well as the planets are connected to the events that occur in nature and in human society and within him. It is one harmony in the structure of Man - Space - Nature where there's nothing unnecessary. The planets' motion and the existence of the human race and other processes within nature are in accordance with the laws of nature.

The main law in space is the rule of law, the principle of harmony. The law of harmony is one for all. Based on this principle it is necessary for the entire world to undergo regular updates. When certain events of qualitative change happen, and after that everything is repeated however at a greater scale. The greater the scale of civilization is, the more it will have to conform with cosmic law or else it'll be a single-minded and primitive the process of development.

The great crises of the 21st century, an era of utter chaos for the entire human race has been linked to the scientifically-based cosmic cycles. Astrologers have identified several phases within the horoscopes of the Earth. One of them, with an estimated duration of 8 million years is the development phase of the Earth that is associated with the motion of the Solar system within the Galaxy. It will end in 2008 which marks the start of the period of transition that is a significant shift on the earth's axis. increasing and decreasing the Earth's surface and causing abrupt changes to vegetation, climate and even flora. There could be some new species of human.

The second macrocycle is a reflection of the the earth's orbit - the axis of precession in which the axis that rotates the Earth in a complex direction is described as the shape of a cone. The period is for 25920 years. This is "a great year", breaking down into twelve "great" (cosmic) months. The cycle has gradual shifts of the sky's starry skies with respect to Earth during one "month" (2160) by 30 degrees, or by the zodiac's one sign. The end of this "month" (precession of the vernal equinox) it is the time to change of epochs and socio-economic patterns.

The cosmic time of Pisces has come to an end, that means that the earth's axis ceases its motion within the constellation of zodiac Pisces. Humanity is in the middle between two great times. The new world is expected to begin around 2003. This is in which it is expected that the Age of Aquarius will enter its final phase. During this time, an entirely new way of advancement of the civilization is being formulated. The events that are preparing for the next period have been taking place for over 200 years. As we approach the 21st century, the more obvious the material, spiritual ecological problem. The dead-end, illusory evolution branches exist, and have ruined many natural connections. The technological and scientific revolutions are responsible for this. The human race will eventually have come back to its roots in the process of reversing how the world's history turns around in a spiral. And before it can be reborn into a brand new nature, the Piscean era has to be completed logically.

2003-2008 is the period that marks ending the cosmic first cycle as well as the start of the second cycle - the age that is the Great Everlasting. The amount of information that accumulates within wildlife is expected to reach its limits. The rhythms of time for the majority of people could change significantly. It will result in a breakdown in the biorhythms of human beings as well as animals, plants and other species, and this could lead to massive genetic mutations among humans and within wildlife, which could accelerate species evolution. An entirely new evolutionary cycle begins. What are the ancient philosophers' views of this century? The writings of Nostradamus: "Humanity will be carried off by the iron toy, that will take over gods by it. It will bring about an invading group of heads-less idiots who will take over those prayers to God inside people's hearts by utterly absurd. Iron birds and their sound will be heard throughout the air. The people will come up with amazing mirrors using that they'll be able talk to and communicate with each other from the distance of a long distance. Iron amphibious transports covered with a cover are set to move along the iron web which will be covering the Earth. The world will be populated with iron vessels that are that will be set to motion "hellfire" as well as steam. A lot of stars will be seen using an optical lens (telescope). The more iron toy are in the world and the more conflicts are likely to be fought, more disunity will be felt by humanity. The greater be the dependence on dictatorship and the greater number of people will be cut off from nature and will begin to seek the revenge they deserve. The air and the land will be polluted, certain seas will die, and lakes be transformed into swamps. "

Civilizational achievements can benefit people, but do not tm Vol

However, for the Zoroastrians and their teachings, which were the precursors to all global religions, the bond between the man and nature was sacred and it was a pious crime to poison the space around it, i.e. four elements, earth, air, water and fire. This represented an assault to harm God spirit. They understood that "a discord in an individual can result in diseases that affect the body and mind that, later can be seen in the natural phenomenon. In particular, The ancients believed conflict within interpersonal relationships as well as in the interaction between humans with nature can lead to natural catastrophes.

OUR time, as seen from the perspective of ancient astrologers is a singular, distinct event that does not have any analogies from the past except for an interval that was 2.5-3 per. many years in the past.

T

XIX - XXI centuries - - the end of time that marked the end for the Great Transition. It is the Great Threshold in the development of civilization has been accompanied by massive crises and challenges. From 15th century, it was reported that our times were in the midst of a crisis: "When the constellations of Pisces and Aquarius come into contact, terrible times will come, and people will become completely different, unlike now." We are at the edge of the final logical step in human history, at the point that our current culture is at its peak.

Mankind has been repeatedly warned in the past time ("Avesta", "Chaldean oracle" 3-4 centuries BC. E.) warnings been issued regarding what was known as the "reserved" (forbidden), end-of-the-road of growth and conflicts. Nostradamus who codified the order of letters within the text, during the 16th century, wrote:

1944 1944 "An unimaginable fire is set to be sparked, bringing

In the morning, death will occur. the flying ship will drop two balls

Two cities of the eastern part of the world are destroyed and turns these cities to D dust. The ruins of the cities will be the traces of those who lived there. " Oi was mistaken for a single year forecasting the disaster that would follow Kherosima and Nagasaki because of the reality that at the time of the blasts, there would be it was predicted that the sun would eclipse and a confluence of the sun. It is also associated with Pluto (nuclear energy spinning in a way that is out of control)+ the moon ties up with Saturn. The prophet also referred at the apocalyptic danger that emanates out of The South Pole of the Earth (the Ozone hole): "At the end of the 20th century diseases and plagues will strike populations."

The lives of people in the past are mystery stories in which myths were realized. The world's history was initially a established scenario that is imaginative, but the result of the game as well as the details of it are not known.

Someone born at a specific date and time determines their amount for the coming period. The fate of the entire world, or of a particular country may depend on this. In the case of example K. Marx was born on the 5th of May, 1818 which was a day of solar eclipse. It wasn't visible in Germany and was only observed across Eastern Europe and Western Siberia in the region between Moscow in the city of Moscow and St. Petersburg. The future of Russia was dependent on the character of Marx and, based on his decision as well as his errors and ill-informed beliefs. persons should never be misled and they are liable for a great obligation. In the year 197 (99 years following his birth Marx that is 9-11 year solar cycles, which started in 1818 with the solar eclipse) A revolution took place in RUSSIA. Events could have evolved differently, but for some reason, the story chose Marxism and the Bolsheviks, and not the Anar-Khistov-Bakinists or the Socialist-Revolutionaries. In principle, it is erroneous and the ideology of one individual led to an extremely powerful *

implications.

One of the principles of astrology is that well-meaning people - caring helpful, compassionate, and hardworking suffer from failing. The basis of this is the concept about "transmigration of souls." In accordance with the laws of Karma that governs how fate of one's life at birth is a cause through his various lives. Every single moment is decided by the law of Karma and has certain consequences either in the present or in the next phase (after physical death, and subsequent birth but within an entirely different body, since the soul will remain immortal) of existence. The fate of a person is caused by the actions performed by

1 E

Human cervical during earlier lives. This is a theory that allows an astrologer to provide the answer to how life can be simpler for one particular person at the mercy of the o l. Godnn

The human being is born multiple times, and the manner of death and the type of life how it's done, is his kids are, and much more, is based on the circumstances in which soul's previous lives were like. So, for instance the event that a child passes away during childhood, it will be an act of remorse for wrongs done by those who have

27

previously had similar Karma. The 100% Law of Karma says: what people do and end up dying (because or because of death at the hands of someone else or because of an accident) reacts to the following existence, and in the event that more violent deaths happen in the past, for an insignificant amount of duration, the entity will suffer similar numbers of deaths. Thus, certain people die prior to the time they were born. So, Karma can be restored and the individual, or his soul inside a new body, is able to continue to grow.

In the end, the subpar postulates of astrology was not enough to cause embarrassment to many prominent scientists who were committed to this fascinating field. The entire world involved with astrology. Kepler (1571-1630). Kepler (1571-1630) "Canon of Medicine" by Ibn Sina (980-1037), an astrological-based medical treatise is not yet published by us. The opinion of amazing scientist of our time -- A, Enshtenn (1879-1955): "Astrology - lch> independently-based science. The author explains many things to us. Through the friendship of drinking, I have gained a lot of knowledge.

I've used it numerous times. "

Chapter 2: Astrogeography And Our Country

The Earth is one integrated living system that is connected to forces from the Cosmos. The reason for this is the principles of astrono

The morphologies of different regions on our planet have special

is a vital function for everyone functions for all of humanity, serving as essential organs that are essential to the body of a human. Every region of the body can be identified using the astrological symbolic and figurative language. Each part of Earth's surface associated with a hefty radiation that is linked to a specific constellation of the zodiac as well as the plaques of the solar system. "This is the field of ASTRO-GEOGRAPHY that investigates the interplay between man with the earth's surrounding space as the same noosphere and with cosmic bodies. Both mankind as well as the Earth as well as the Cosmos constitute a part of the cosmic sphere.

The cosmic grid is where India, Tibet, and in addition, the Indian ethnos are the functions as the center of Earth and feed its people by bringing ideas. Western Eastern Europe and above all, Great Britain (in the west) as well as Japan (in East) as well as in the east, Far East carry the function of both the right and left humans' lungs, and are one living thing. Indonesia is hands. Africa has the legs. Kamchatka can be male and Mediterranean as well as the Black Sea the female genital organs. In the Black Sea, the ethnos, states, and civilizations emerge constantly.

The core of our civilisation is that of the Cordillera mountains (in South America -

the Andes) that stretch across 18 thousand kilometres. The Cordillera Mountains are the centre of the connection between cosmic energy and earth, and the spinal cord is in sync with the solar plexus of the human body. This is huge cosmodrome within the Pasca desert, a place of palaeocontact that provided essential information to the human race. Through this massive ramp that Earth communicates with its counterpart to another planet within the star system. Five nerve centers located on the spine that project out on the surface of Earth, correspond to the locations where the oldest civilizations were founded several thousand years back. Additionally, the Tierra of Fuego is the central point of cosmic fire within the spine of the human. Every region on the Earth is connected to any or the Zod Naka constellations: Kit the th Capricorn,

Eastern Europe and Western Siberia - Aquarius, Australia -and Strelets, Central Europe (especially Germany) -- Aries. Northern Europe - Taurus, North America - Gemini, India - Virgo, Great Britain and Japan - Libra, South America - Leo, Palestine and Arabia - Pisces, Medium. East, Middle and Southeast Asia - Scorpio, Africa - Cancer. Additionally, there are seven areas of the Earth that have planetary cycles. Like, for instance, Western Europe depends on the impact of the Sun and its past is a reflection of 11-year sun's activity.

The locations of the stars in the sky can have different effects on particular areas of the earth's surface.

Earth (moles and warts within your body) These are the causes of them.

Highly and informatively filled with information and energy. They are isn't a lot of the same in the world of Earth they are referred to as "good", attractive, in which life was once enjoyed there, in which aliens and people (luminous as well as flying saucers) are attracted. In the region of Russia These include Kamchatka, Sakhalin, the Crimea (formerly an island), Baikal, Ladoga as well as Baikal, Ladoga and the Volga as well as the Don rivers, and the Perm Region, the territory of the Kursk and Voronezh magnetic anomalies. The human race from these regions feeds off vitality-giving energy. If these places have been ruined, the Earth begins to seek revenge against the human race (terrible winds, flooding rivers, forests and even people, massive seismic waves, and earthquakes (including earthquakes in regions with low risk of seismic activity). There is no chance that there's no earthquakes occurring in Antarctica and Antarctica, which is where

now almost no people.

The great epoch of Fisher that was marked through the births of many great individuals (Jesus Christ, Mahomet, etc.) and have had the greatest impact on those who lived during this time, is close to its conclusion. The region comprised of Arabia, Egypt, Palestine and Palestine, that is home to the functions that the liver performs (a organ for forming blood and also one of the most biochemically clean parts within the body) as well as gall bladder of the Earth, is connected with the constellation of the zodiac, Pisces. In 157 BC. The year was 157 BC. In 157 BC. Oe., the time when the era of Pisces was beginning The cosmic ray directed towards this region of the earth. Thus, it was here that two world religions

(Christianity as well as Islam) emerged and spread across the world with two half-rings.

In the 2 millennia-year ago, was the heart of Earth civilization. In this region of Earth numerous nations established superethnos that have been able to preserve ancient practices up to the present. Christianity Islam and Judaism. But, slowly, as the age of Aquarius is near the end of Aquarius, that "place of power" weakens and shifts from Palestine towards Russia during 2021. In the event of leaving Israel and it is the Jews are a hindrance to this even though this area is the heart of human civilization is not occupied for more than 2 millennia. If Israel is not divided in Samaria (Shomron), Galilee (Galil) and Judea and Judea, it'll remain a great place to live to stay for quite a while. The Age of Pisces is leaving as well as the eight-million year period during the evolution of Earth as well as humanity follows it.

*

The heart of the world's civilization in the early 20th century will be Russia as the country that ancient astrologers considered to be a major focus it. It was mentioned in "Avesta" as the country of Jair. The Greeks described it as a nation of Hyperboreans, or Cimmerians and the Europeans called it Scythia, Tartary, Muscovy.

From the beginning the area that is Eastern Europe and Western Siberia along with the people who reside in it, are closely associated with

This constellation is Aquarius symbolizes the distinction between light and darkness, of the gross from delicate, and the true from true from the false. The 2160 year-old period of Aquarius and is characterized by the expansion of consciousness as it begins. It is generally believed that Aquarius is marked by many different kinds of surprise. In the future, the future is unique, and its people will be distinguished through determined actions and changes of thinking. The symbol for Uranus that governs this astronomical constellation it represents a bolt of lightning which cannot be anticipated or could not hit everywhere.

Aquarius talks about aspirations mostly from the spiritual world. For him, material interest is not the primary concern. Individuals born under this sign are very friendly and possess imaginative talents, extraordinary ability to laugh, get it right and a vivid imagination. They don't like any kind of discipline; they aren't keen on binding themselves with obligations, and they of the time, don't earn a cent and don't even care about at all. The majority of them have the ability to see the future, or the capacity to predict the future, and provide an example of faith and endurance for the people in their vicinity. These people suffer from the monotony, routine and intangibility of the tasks they are required to do. If they're interested or need to do their best, not only in their own interest, but to help the sake of a loved one, they'll be diligent and always be there

For help, give them their last contact details.

It's on the terrain of Russia that a new people is expected to emerge, and a brand tradition and culture will come back. The start of the Aquarian period coincides with the start in the cycle cosmic that will run for 8 million years. Thus, the area that is under the sign of Aquarius is going to become a center where power is generated, and will be the beginning of the next civilization for the future eight million years. We can therefore claim that Russia will be the world's capital in the near future. Russian will become a worldwide language in the same way as today English. There will be people who want to learn it in the event that civilizations change completely, where our country will be the one planet where people have a decent existence. All the rest of Earth will be undergoing traumatic changes that are hard to imagine.

It's no accident to note that it was within the Southern Urals in which Zarathustra, the Prophet Zarathustra was born nearly

27 centuries back, that the first teachings of Zarathustra were made.

concerning the principle of spirituality in man, and also the doctrine about the spiritual principle in man and the teachings of "Avesta", in which the moral laws were originally defined as principles from the Cosmos. The Aryan populace is the genealogical Träger of this teaching as well as the spirit and tradition.

Based on astrogeography, both according to astrogeography, East European and West Siberian Plains are the brains of Earth's brain. They are separated in terms of the two hemispheres is the Ural Mountains (Khairati), that are the major centers on the globe. It is thought to be the center of light and reason, and its function in Russia is distribution of the mind.

across the globe's civilisation. Russia is the security guardian of our minds however, just like the schizoid or syphilitic it is degrading because of tragic events, the effects that we've cleaned up for the past more than 73 years. However, there's an opportunity to restore the health that the brain. If the brain goes out of existence all the humans on Earth will be without a specific mentality. It is possible to live without having a brain, but your actions of people will not be justified, and mankind can only perform the most basic duties.

At first, there were four races living on Earth and the earliest inhabitants (the blue races) emerging from Antarctica and being transported by space. There are several undiscovered continents in our world: Atlantis, Pacific (in the Pacific), Antarctica, Lemuria (Indian Ocean) and

Arctis which was a warm and sweltering island that ended up dying tens of millions of years in the past. And then on Earth there was a uniform climate due to the fact that it rotated as though sitting on its side.

The basis of our European civilization is derived from the earliest Aryans who were once a part of the Arktide that is currently (at the very bottom of Arctic Ocean) crossed by the Lomonosov and Mendeleev Ridges. In the book "Avesta" and the collection of Indian myths "Rig Veda", the Ancient Aryans, who were the ancestral ancestors of the Indo-European tribes mostly Slavs, came to Eurasia through the Ural Mountains, settled in two rings of Eastern Europe and Western Siberia Then, through three rivers they went towards Yugdo Tibet, Himalayas and Altai. For the people of ancient times, one of the works from"Avesta

"Avesta" - "Bund-Hishna" (creation of the universe) promises a new beginning following a time of massive turmoil, and states: "The Earth's axis will move and indicate the East and merge the three branches of the Jair tree cut down and destroyed (Russian, Ukrainian and Belarusian people) ". The connection is expected to take place immediately following 2008 and last through the next time of Aquarius.

Prior to the dawn of the Aquarian period, mankind particularly those Aryan populations that resided in our nation had to face hardships. these hardships could have been averted by the majority of mankind was not unable to remember its spiritual origins. As an example, in Russia there would have been no satanic governing when, after the advent of Christianity towards the close in the 10th century the deep roots of Russian ethnicity and the ancient customs derived from traditional teachings from the early Aryans and pagan religions, could not have been destroyed and if the Russian populace could have a chance to resist the destructive effects of the alien ideologies and prejudices Furthermore, Christianity has played an important part in Russian the past, is also derived from the Zoroastrian doctrines from the Avesta. There is no coincidence that Jesus Christ, up to 30 years old had a study in Persia along with adherents of Zarathustra as well as in India from healers and yogis. When he returned back to Palestine, Christ preached the doctrines of the Avesta even though they didn't align with the commands of the prophets from the Old Testament.

There was a reason why Nostradamus was averse toward the Russian country, and as an astrologer didn't honor as an astrologer is required to be objective and impartial. He referred to the inhabitants on our land "Tartars" (i.e., "people of Tartar or Hell"). He often regretted the fact that these apparently barbaric group needed to take on many nations and establish a huge empire.

The 16th century was the time when Nostradamus expressed his joy in a clear and unmistakable way:

"After 400 years. (I.e. in the start at the beginning of the twentieth century) in the country that is Hyperboreans (Tartary), Hyperboreans (Tartary) the world's largest change will begin to take place during October. It is a revolution that many believe to be one of the biggest ever seen in the history of Earth. It will begin to erupt at the end of 2017 (1917) when there will be the highest amount of eclipses that will occur of the

Sun as well as the Moon and their total is seven. The life on Earth is going to cease to grow easily and will plunge into vast darkness. "

L918

"I see the royal thrones crumbling, As the human hurricane overthrows all of them, the republic will be made worse by the crown, And the red and white are cruel deception" ..

An extremely precise picture of the revolution of October was sketched:

"A brand new religion has been made by a dogma. every spectacle is a grand fraud.

Beasts of noble measurement size,

As for evil, it is the good is thrown at us. "

He also predicted his prediction that "In the state of the barbarians, most of the court nobility will be sent to the scaffold." Around the time of the beginning in the year under the Bolshevik regime the writer said:

"Autumn 1917 and winter 1918 will be peaceful, and in the spring and summer of 1918 there will be tremendous changes, the fall of kingdoms and great earthquakes, the greatest calamities will begin that have never happened on Earth." In another quatrain an extremely soft image of J. Stalin (Dzhugashvili) is presented:

"I am scared of the unidentified third king of the inscrutable and savage, snowy, country

The other members of his group are killed by him. And in his old age is the only place that hell can protect him. "

"Sons are going to rebel against their parents, temples will be destroyed, the people are going to start eating one another and terrible devastation will ensue and horrors will be witnessed all around. It will be the new Babylon that will be filled with prostitution barbaric and disgusting duz Vnon destruction, which is going to cause suffering to the entire Earth. "

The post-revolutionary Russia:

"Snowstorms storms, rains, and rebellions at the Arctic zero

When people turn into worse monsters

This will transforms into prison. The "Do not kill" law will be enforced to Anathema.

#

"The the new Xerxis Atilla will rise, that will destroy the people who are in the grip of a terribly red sect that is among the most bloody. Then there will be devastating destruction for many nations around this evil state. The most harrowing of them all will be the citizens of Tartarpi that will be forced endure the oppression. The world will be able to survive two conflict. The days of the human race will be cut short And let us make sure that we do never leave a living soul here on earth should we are to obey the Lord

Have lived to see this day. This catastrophe will last seven months and 73 years. "

It follows that the 70 years of Satanic rule that was the rule of Bolsheviks -- known as the track of the Antichrist -- will be ended with a sigh in the months of May and June 1991. In a rage and scream, the crowd will hurl Lenin from the podiums. Now we're in the end of this horror, since"the "socialist system" no longer exists. The Soviet Union, which had no legal right to exist as a fake, unnatural state that is a part of the boundaries of time and space is eroding. Any unscientific ideology can be destroyed however, not astrology founded on observations and experiences over thousands of years.

#

But, Nostradamus adds that "for a long time the Hyperborean people will heal their wounds and not only will reason be able to break the deadlock." This is why you shouldn't celebrate the coming conclusion of the disaster that afflicted our country. "Although the earth Mars has come to an end, before the completion of its revolving door, the whole process will begin in the future, so let people living in northern lands Northern Land not be happy at the prospect of getting rid of the oppression that was imposed by the antichrist's wrathful times because new catastrophes and new turmoils are in store for their arrival, while the thriving earth might turn into

The desert. However, God will be kind towards them. And, even though Satan's people Satan are trying to cover themselves with other clothing They are not they who are the National Assembly will succeed. "

The French psychic R. Nehru (XV century) The teacher of Nostradamus said that (blessed will be) the one born at the line between two times in the history of this country as he'll have grace marks on him.

"And he. is to be born "in the city of northernity, among the northern population that is

People of prophets, poets as well as martyrs ". R. Nehru believed in metapsychosis as well as the karmic pathway of spirituality. "

The prophet also spoke of new cities that are emerging in the Nordic nation, that may come into existence later and then be revived.

#

1702 1702 "Venice will rise up on the North Sea,

It will be a city that rises over the dead water. there will be a majestic cat sitting in the throne of tartar will raise the banners of victory conflict. "

It is Petersburg A city that was founded in the swamps "the cat * s real cat" is Peter I, who was depicted as an animal. Victory War - the Northern War (1700-1721) featuring

By of the Swedes. Thus, the prediction of Nostradamus was clearly realized. It was also in this city in the north where, due to its great potential and immense power R. Nehru predicted his return exactly 500 years following his passing away (that was during the 90s of the 20th century) This person is also a good forecaster.

Chapter 3: Planet Parade - The Mystery Of Our Time

The time is now, and there's a shift in cosmic eras

the formation of the planets. In the first sector of the night sky there is the most massive group of planets that repeats

Every 480-500 years occurs each year the Grand Parade of the Planets. The small planet parade is held every 180 to 190 years.

The current parade of the planets, all distant planets were centered within three constellations: Scorpio, Sagittarius and Capricorn. The first parade of planets took place in 1982. The result is the condensing of events, rapid acceleration of massive shifts, which cause social turmoil as well as a paradigm shift in the world. All of our universe is interconnected and the events of

Cosmos coincide with the events in the world on Earth at one point or the other, reflecting the latter.

In the past, during one of the Planet Parades (2500 years ago) There was an explosion of Persian ethnos that took over the Earth through Greece as well as China. After that, there was the beginning of the Greek ideas and the philosophy from the Buddha (623-544 BC CE) as well as the Kun-tzu era (551-479 BC). The planets' dazzling parade was during the first century AD. e.--

The birth of Christianity The birth of Christianity, the conflicts of conquering The Ancient World, the heyday of the Roman Empire and ancient culture. The planetarium parade towards the close 15th century marked the start of the Renaissance in Western Europe, the liberation of Russia from the Mongols.

The beginning of the period of geographical events 1492, the peak of the Parade of the Planets -and the discovery of America 1497, the first discovery of the southern route that leads to India through Vasco da Ga my. Portuguese Vasco da Ga my. 1517 was the year of the Reformation (M. Luther).

The spectacle of planets that took place in the 20th century started around 1982. In actual fact, there are many distant planets from the solar system (Saturn,

Neptune, Uranus, Pluto, Proserpina - 10 planets which have been orbiting the Sun for over 500 years) that are in the constellations of Scorpio and Sagittarius are now in the constellations since 1977. As per astrology this zodiac signification of Scorpio is a sign of the Middle East (Iran, Iraq, Afghanistan, Pakistan * , Azerbaijan) and Central Asia (without

Kazakhstan). In this part of Earth where political turmoil began to develop one after another.

1977. Military government coup in Pakistan. Zya-ul-Hak was dismissed on 3. Bh? Tto.

1978 1979 - Afghanistan, Marxist N. Taraki took over Presidy *, and M. Daud.

1979 - The Islamic Revolution in Iran led by R. Ho-meini.

11980 (as of 11980) Iraqi leader S. Hussein began the eight-year-old

War in the Middle East with Iran.

1979 - Two military coups in Afghanistan. The government of puppet B. Karmal was brought by Russian bayonets.

In 1979 in 1979, The Soviet Union joined the development of events and exacerbated its internal crises. The fiery cauldron just began and will continue to increase due to the fact that Pluto symbolizes the untamed factor in the manifesting of natural and social forces "will calm down" only around 1995. The war currently raging within the Middle East will last another 2 years. Meanwhile, Saddam Hussein (born 04/04/1937) remains in power.

-- Taurus as well as other revolutionary ideologues: Cromwell, Robespierre, Ulyanov (Lenin), Hitler, Khomeini). Taurus is angry and it's difficult to take away his blood, and that of those who are Iraqis S. Hussein will be shed until the violence ceases. Following the explosion that was reported in the Rovno nuclear power station (1992) the man is likely to be killed, or have the chance to flee. Then they will have to deal in a confrontation with "leader of the Libyan revolution," M. Gaddafi who was cursed since long ago. He is facing a very difficult fate, and virtually none of the chance to survive. The star constellation Scorpio there is no an open planet Proserpina is the one that regulates quality of transformations, structural changes and genetic changes. Scorpio has died, but revives, however at the highest level which is why it's better not to disturb the planet. In 1979 when The USSR "pulled" to a long-running war during the Middle

East. It's no accident since the Soviet authority was established under the influence of Scorpio and the first-class"Skor-Inon" valet, which is the first class "Skor-Inon" valet, which declares SITI and above all it's destruction-("scorched earth" strategies) Self-majored. constantly searching for adversaries. It's characterized by limits and the determination to conquer the world (the absurd notion that"the world revolution") "world revolution"). It was created from 1917 within the independent, free and unpredictable nation of Aquarius and is foreign to the people of our time. In addition, among the rulers of Cosmos there were two individuals elected to the Politburo the CPSU Central Committee who were accountable for the Soviet military intervention in Afghanistan namely the principal ideology-setter M. Suslov (born November 8th on 19th November, 1902) as well as the Minister in charge of "defense" D. Ustinov (30.10.1908) - - both were born under the zodiac sign of Scorpio. Also, L. I. Brezhnev (12/19/1906 -- Sagittarius) in the year 1906 did not have any responsibility for anything since he had passed into senility.

insane, didn't understand everything, except for the medals that are distinct from the jacket in the brilliance. Then in

1979, a thing happened that wasn't supposed to occur, and yet could have been done to prevent it. The process of developing irreversible events started, and the country began to take a new turn into the pit of disaster. Pakistan, Iran, India then became involved in Afghan incidents, and the procedure will continue for quite a while. The 1990s saw violent events took place occurred in Uzbekistan, Turkmenistan, and Tajikistan continue to take place that will create the remaining points on this nexus.

1982 was the year that began the mysterious Parade of the Planets. The manifestation of this was evident naturally in the nation formed in the constellation of Sagittarius (30L2.1922) and Scorpio (November 8th 1918) and should become predominant in the world of the next century. From Russia that the human crises will begin and will impact every country in the globe. Spiritual or material change that will be taking place around the globe will begin in Russia.

In our nation as well as around the globe is in a way an occurrence of humanity's reaction to the changing of cosmic eras, as well as it is also the Grand Parade of Planets, which began exactly was on the 13th of November 1982. The entire Soviet Union "said goodbye" to L. Brezhnev, who passed away 7-9.11 .1982. It is possible to say that he died according to the plan. In the funeral of Secretary General was destroyed by unusual circumstances, including three alarming signs.

Astrologer of ancient times. In the end, however, sign, symbol, or randomness are the result of laws the manifestation of laws which are not yet understood by them.

1. First indication - what was the way in which the king of a massive empire to be buried? The coffin shook into the ground, and he fell off the straps with an eerie sound. It is believed that at this moment terrible, fatal forces appeared. 2. The coffin is to be lowered into the pit. Remia is an indication that the person who died will be able to draw each of the people who were together, and lastly, the third sign is a massive amount of thieves that took off from all over the world into Red Square and drowned out by their terrible croaksreproductions. Raven shadows cast over people. Consequently they're attracted to an abundance of bodies which means that death was not a solo act. The birds fly in a group to rape -- an event of commemoration, which signifies that the rape won't be a solitary event.

In the days before the burial of Leonid Brezhnev in the crypt, the bottom of his coffin was ripped off. Then, in the Hall of Columns, the lower part of the coffin was crushed by an iron plate. Do rotten nails happen to get stuck? In all likelihood, this could be a clue - there was a reason why others figures didn't drop off the top of the coffin. However, the funeral occurred at the beginning of

The Parade of Planets where the night sky played a role in the appearance of these bizarre indicators.

Then came then the "five-year lush funeral" - "mor" among the General Secretaries as well as members of the Politburo. The process of clearing the stage of historical events started. 1983-85: preparations for the glory days of the Parade of the Planets. The period lasted 2.5 years before that the Great Parade of the Planets began to gain momentum. I (1682) was the first, and prior to this, the link between Pluto with Proserpina was discovered during the Kulikovo Battle (1380). These events are pivotal in the development of Russia.

In March 1985 when the key procedure (perestroika) was initiated, triggered through the changing of the Kremlin head. This was exactly

at the time that Gorbachev was elected at the time, one could discern the cosmic symbolism that he was the king, as it wasn't an accident that the individual born in the zodiac symbol of Pisces was the first to be born to be born in the nation of Aquarius. It happened due to the fact that it was in his time when the era that were the time of Pisces and Aquarius as well as that the Age of Pisces must be spiritually and logically completed under the rule of men who was Pisces and Aquarius. This would be the summation of it all,

Mikhail Gorbachev (Fish) became General Secretary on the 11th of March of 1985. It was the point of the meeting with Pluto with Proserpina. The very last day of the Age of Pisces, In an unequal fight in which he defeated an individual born in the Aquarius sign Aquarius Grigory Romanov (02/07/1923) in the final round by only one voice, that of the A. Gromyko (Cancer) the constellation of nz, which was included in a trine along with fish .

The Age of Pisces and the Age of Aquarius will long remain in close contact with one with each other. In our nation, the conflict continues at a higher level. The famous Boris Yeltsin (born 1.02.1931) replaced G. Romanov.

Aquarius was the very first position in Russia and was the most important

Soviet republics.

In the year 11987 Yeltsin was degraded and forced to walk on party members but he could not be killed. He was a deputy president in 1989. was elected USSR the people's deputy of Moscow In 1990, he was elected the President of Russia and in 1991 it is possible that he will become the president of the USSR in case the Union continues to exist. The most important fight in the conflict between Yeltsin and Gorbachev will not be over yet and will continue for a long time, however the most intense fights are likely to occur in the months of September and October 1990, during the sessions of the USSR Supreme Soviet then between March and April of 1991 (perhaps from June to June 1991 at which point suffering of evil empires is over - that's for the USSR.) The 11991 election will be difficult for both the leaders (to an extent) - for Gorbachev and the USSR).

and which will weaken) which will weaken, and in the United States, the most sharpest of poly can be found * 24

Ha, however it would be best if the two heads stay in politics for some time working together. If not, a single person who is able to defeat an opponent could take over the country.

The war will last until the year 1994, at which point the amazing conjunction that is Uranus and Neptune is expected to occur. It will not be a huge bloodshed in the event that both continue to be at the helm.

The power of Russia (a country that falls under the signification of Aquarius) must not be placed in the hands of a single person which only causes extremes. To allow to allow the Aquarius system to remain stable it is imperative to have two leaders within the social structure, and 2

forces, 2 positions.

The signification of Russia The Russian sign - Aquarius is home to two vessels: an amphora filled with alive water as well as an urn that has an empty one. If there is only one vessel left then the water is likely to become stagnant. In the event that a combination of our nation's extreme conditions and normal growth can it be sustained, M. S. Gorbachev as a skilled and slippery fish is able to emerge from any collision. Raisa Gorbachev (Capricorn born 5 January 1932) is not in the main the cause of our problems However, her birth date is close to the birthday of the spouse of the Romanian ruler Helena Ceausescu.

In the event that M. Gorbachev survives a extremely difficult spring in 1991 (B. Yeltsin's job is more favourable) He will "calmly" sit on the Kremlin the throne until (he will reach his final peak in the year 1995, after which his popularity is likely to increase as a result of his economic standing). There is a 70% chance that

Gorbachev is likely to survive the disastrous year that he had for himself in 1991 However, in order for that to be the case, the leader must change his own environment. Most likely the Prime Minister N. Ryzhkov will resign during the months of January-March 1991. Yeltsin won't be in a position to pull Russia through the grave crisis, but the Russian leader will be able to bring in three new leaders to succeed his predecessor, and he will be their model. When 1996 comes around, Uranus is in into the constellation Aquarius, Yeltsin will leave his political sphere and will be replaced by Gorbachev.

However, in no way will one ever shed blood of the rulers of the country for so long many years. This is because when blood is the only thing that can give birth to revenge and blood, the chain of pogroms and violence commences, and therefore there is nothing that can be done to improve the situation. Anyone who claims that the blood of the roses is in a stable state and is not able to be considered a positive factor. Usurpers need to leave peacefully and not allow bloody incidents to occur again. As an example for instance, the Romanian "genius of the Carpathians" N. Chaushesku was born on the 22nd of January 1918, the day of the moon's eclipse. Sun in January. Then, in January of 1990, there was a second moon eclipse Sun (exactly 72 years of age at the time - a death time) which was later to prove fatal to N. Ceausescu . Additionally that in the month of December 1989, an alliance between Saturn and Neptune started, and occurred each year for 36 years, that is, the killing of the ruler who was supreme (1953 - the murder of Dzhugashvili-Stalin between 1917 and 1918 - the killing of the families that belonged to Nicholas II Romanov, 1881 The murder of Alexander II " the liberator of the peasants "),

Additionally, Socialist Romania was founded on the 12th of December, 1947 on the exact day that was the Soviet Union. In Romania the stars signalled the bloody incidents in December 1989. And these took place. If H, Ceausescu was not executed, Romania would very quickly emerge from the turmoil. N. Ceausescu was brutally killed, and without trial, which laid the groundwork for his cult of personality and Ceausescu's national chanting. hero of Romania into this century. So, there's an extremely high risk of a new military entering into Romania as well as the rise to power of a brand new dictator. For I. Iliescu (born 03.03.1930, Pisces), 1990-1992 is a traumatic time as a violent end is in his future at the close in 1992.

One of the effects of the planetarium parade at the close to the century of 20th was an accident that occurred in the Chernobyl nuclear power station, that occurred in the year 1986. The in the same year, Halley's comet was en route to Earth (it was believed to have been as a comet in China for two thousand years BC as well as in Greece for a period of 11,000 years BC). It was seen before the collapse of Ancient Rome (476), the capture of England by the Normans as well as the Battle of Hastings (1066) and the 4th Crusade (1202), the defeat of Constantinople by the Turks (1453). and the trail of the comet pointed toward the location where events of great difficulty were later on. Comets are, in the past, considered "God's sign",

Unpredictability is a factor that can disrupt people's lives.

The last time that this "shaggy star" appeared in 1909-1910, which pointed to Eastern Europe and the Northern Hemisphere overall. In 1912-1913, the time of war between Balkan nations and Turkey In 1914, in 1914, the 1st World

War broke out in 1917, triggering the revolutionary era in Russia and the complete eradication of the old social order. On April 11th, in 1986 Halley's comet travelled within close proximity to Earth and again pointed with its head toward the territories in European Russia.

Nostradamus said that the coming of the Comet (in 1936) brought 7 new illnesses "carrying the star of Revelation on its tail." This was no accident that in 1981, just as the comet reached the limit of its Solar System, AIDS was recognized as the disease that destroys human immunity against all diseases. In 1985, it was found that T-leukemia is and blood cells are affected in a mysterious way, and with a much worse form.

More than typical. in 1990, Uzbekistan identified the fungus, that is known as

Patilomycosis Variola. It can affect the muscles as well as various other systems vital to our body. In the last few years, a strange disease emerged in the nations in Asia in the form of which a small percentage of young men quickly pass away in the night. Chapter 8 in the Revelation in the Revelation of John The Theologian (Apocalypse) the following disaster is explained: "The third angel sounded as a massive shining star fell from the heavens that was burning as a light and falling on one third of the streams and rivers of water. The star's name was Wormwood ("Chernobyl" or "Chernobyl" in Ukrainian) And three-quarters of the water transformed into wormwood as well as a lot of the inhabitants died in the water because it were bitter. "

Comet Halley in 1986 was rotated with its tail in the constellation Sagittarius in which the most moons were accumulated during the month as well. Sagittarius means Ukraine (Taurus) represents the sign of the 8th (the 8th house is known as the place of death and transformation). It was also in the constellation Sagittarius on the 24th of April the lunar eclipse took place in 1986. The moon shattered Pluto on that day, the closest it could get to the Earth as it could be, and it's Pluto as it is connected to elements, unlimited energy, particularly nuclear energy. Similar eclipses were observed on the 16th of July, 1945 (Alamogordo Desert, New Mexico, USA) and also during

Other big explosions. Additionally to that, the Sun was within the constellation Taurus that was a sign of the city's outskirts.

So, right after the 24th of April, this horrific incident was set to happen, and unfortunately, it happened during the night of April 25-26, 1986.

Astrologer P. P. Globa predicted the year 1981 that in April of 1986, in Ukraine (or perhaps in Transcaucasia) there would be A nuclear disaster local to the area could occur with serious effects for people as there are a number of analogies to similar incidents

In the nuclear power plant it was. The comet, the demon of God has always been a signal for things that have not ever been analogized. Furthermore, Nostradamus predicted these terrible occasions: 1986 "The the tail of a terrifying comet will strike the Earth;

Hair as well as skin and eyes are in complete fear from the deeps of Borisfen

". (Borysfen Borisfen - the old Greek name for the River Dnieper).

The devastating effects of the nuclear accident in Chernobyl's Chernobyl nuclear power plant the resulting accidents, and other issues at nuclear power plants are expected to be felt for the next 18 years, and for 10 to 11 days (the Saros cycle), which are linked with the lunar eclipse cycle which started when the lunar eclipses again co-occurred with the Chernobyl catastrophe. After 18 years, the effects of the catastrophe are neutralized or shifted to a different scale. Chernobyl will, obviously is not going to occur again, however radioactive leaks and the threat of nuclear war will not go away. It will occur on May 4, 2004, to commemorate the birthday of Karl Marx. It is a good idea to note that the ascending signs in his horoscope i.e. the defining

The fate of the planet was Aquarius as well as with the sunrise angle at 24 degrees. This signifies our country of origin.

In the case of Belarus the nuclear power stations located within the territory of neighboring countries could risk the lives of those in neighboring territories. It is possible for them to occur at Ignalpna NPP (Lithuania) and most importantly the region of Ukraine and, first in all, on the Rovno NPP (Kuznetsovsk which is located about 50 km to the from the Ukrainian-Belarusian border) in the year 1992.

The year, or the time at which it begins year, it is the time that "feat" of Chernobyl will occur again - an accident or explosion an reactor leaking radiation however on a lesser magnitude than 1986. Additionally, in 1994-95 it is possible that the South-Ukrainian NPP is located in the region between Odessa and Nikolayev may blast off. This can be explained by the reality that Pluto is within the constellation of Scorpion which is threatening Taurus which could impact power stations within Ukraine and in the vicinity such as Novovoronezh NPP (but not Smolensk NPP).

The building of the Khmelnitsky NPP was started with a tragic timing it poses particular risk in Eastern Europe. Like the Rivne NPP was built on the eclipse of a sun at the most dangerous spot. The station will explode immediately as when it's activated. It is therefore wise to avoid repeating the horrible test. However, the risk can be avoided by putting off the building of new NPPs and stopping, shutting the "dismantling operating NPPs with threatening characteristics / In 1998-1990, it is possible that people will give up on the" peace-loving atom that is present in every home "and may think about different issues that are more crucial to humanity.Knowing this, it's imperative to unite all resources, to prevent horrible incidents.

An accident of major magnitude at a plant for chemical production (probably located in Vitebsk or Polotsk) may be a possibility in north Belarus during 1994. There is nothing to menace Minsk however Belarus is facing serious problems.

Chapter 4: The Soviet Union At The Crossroad Of Epoch

"THE FATE OF BELARUS"

Belorussia. It is known as the "good land" located under the constellation of Capricorn. The land is controlled by the Moon and is which is associated with abundance of water. It also affects the landscape that is lake-marshy in Belarus. The satellite (satellite from the Earth) describes the characteristics that characterize the population of Belarus as a traditionalism, apathy, passiveness, slow growth as well as some indecisiveness, lack equilibrium, and emotional compliance particularly for aid of larger nations.

It was during Capricorn (the indication of Belarus) where Belarus was born. Parade of the Planets should conclude in 1994, at the time that Neptune and Uranus joined within this constellation. this was the time when the areas that are associated with this particular sign of the Zodiac were to be fully evident - they're now getting ready for the forthcoming eruption. Capricorn is known for its extraordinary determination and perseverance. He will do anything to attain his goal. Moon provides the necessary an element

In the end, there is a lot of emotion and vagueness - however, when a particular goal has been set, you must not deviate to the goal. Furthermore to that, in Belarus the swamps connected to the moon shouldn't be depleted, as the Belarusian country will shrink to a minimum and the characteristics that are characteristic of the lunar world are lost to people: poetry and sensibility. In July of 1990 The Belarusian Parliament adopted the Declaration of State

Sovereignty of the Republic during a very opportune moment, as the Sun and the vast majority of planets were located in the constellation Leo which is a symbol of transition and death in that particular Capricorn system. Additionally, the event was immediately following the eclipse of the sun on 07/22/1990. In Lithuania (Cancer) in the country of Cancer, the legislature was declared independent on the 11th of March of 1990, an event that was considered to be a significator because the Sun was under the zodiac sign of Pisces (Pisces and Cancer are watermarks). and Jupiter as also known as "star of kings," was located in the constellation Cancer. In the month of August, 1990 Jupiter changed into the constellation of Leo and this meant difficult time for Belarus through the year 1990. However, the more difficult the circumstances in Lithuania will be, the more comfortable it will be to be in Belarus because Cancer as well as Capricorn are the two most prominent constellations.

opposite zodiac signs.

In the year 1991 (the time that was the year of the White Ram) from 1993 was a devastating crisis that erupted within Belarus and throughout the nation (Nostradamus: "The White Baran will carry the Hyperborean people through the abyss that will last 3 years"). The years ahead will be a chaotic one of famine and cold destruction. Additionally, it is expected that martial law will be declared in certain areas in the USSR. Belarus will be confronted with a number of shifts in its economy, ideologies and the environment. However, Belarus is likely to be impacted by the current crisis in a smaller way than other parts within the Soviet Union.

In the year 1991, as a result of the lunar eclipse within the constellation of Capricorn in the constellation under which Belarus is situated, three new individuals will become known within the country One of them will be its leader. He'll be a powerful man, yet it is likely that he will do better than the current hetman of Ukraine and will be relying on the alliance between Cossack foremen. As that the Moon is a female-oriented planet and the Holy Virgin Mary is the patron saint of Belarus The opposition is expected to be a significant factor in the politics of Belarus and be visible at the end of November 1991 or the early part of 1992 following another eclipse of the Moon within the constellation of Capricorn. In 1995, the opposition is headed by the third most powerful person and will be led by the president of Belarus and his rival lot will be on the line in the political future of Belarus.

The year 1992 will begin at the time that Jupiter is in the constellation Virgo and the lives of Belarus becomes easier. an era of national and the cultural revival will commence that will last for 3 years. Furthermore, lunar cycles can have an impact significant on Belarusians living in Belarus. So, the impacts from the Declaration (1990) regarding sovereignty, which was adopted at an unfavorable time and will continue to be felt over the next 18 years (the cycles of moon's phases) because of the total eclipse of the Sun 07/22/1990. To break or slow down this cycle it is imperative to either adopt the Law concerning the sovereignity of Belarus or modify the Declaration as well. It's recommended to do so at a time when the Sun is located in the constellation in Taurus (best for the best), Virgo or Capricorn. With the aid of symbols astrological tones You can define

The best method to select determine the most probable future forecast.

Belarus, as a quiet territory, expects a very

Slow development. It is expected to slow down until the time when its leaders set the clear and consistent objectives for development for the country. Belarus isn't in the process of awaiting demise or extinct however, it is expected to stay through the crisis for a lengthy time while protecting its forces. The year 1993 will be the time when Belarus may conclude that many things have gone wrong and there's no more to hold back for. However, in 1994, Belarus' economic condition country will dramatically improve.

Statehood is a process within Belarus is more difficult than other republics. When 1994 arrives, Belarus will attain its an arduous process of becoming independent in the form of a state with a presidency that will confer some advantages over the previous status, though this may not be the ultimate benefit. But, Belarus as an independent country will only last for a brief period of time (14-18 years) as in the early century XXI, it will be part of the single Slavic (Aryan) superethnos.

The Capricorn system is always led by an administrator who takes charge of everything happening within the republic. If his beloved is killed, Capricorn dissolves. The chief, who is a person with the formal (authority) and actual (he could become president) authority, will be able to appear in Belarus between 1995 and 1996 following the huge union in 1994 between Uranus and Neptune within the constellation known as Capricorn. The work of the chief will commence in late 1991 when, getting elected into the republican legislature for the first time, will be able to identify himself. He will also reveal his true self during 1993. It is likely that he will be President in 1995. The presidency lasting 7 years. This is during the reign of Saturn, who governs Capricorn. He will be one born under the sign of Capricorn or in Taurus. Taurus. To attract the attention of the current leaders of Belarus: P. Masherov (born on February 26, 1918. Fish) The man was in logical terms complete the time period of Pisces within the borders of Belarus However, the sudden death of the ruler prevented.

In the end, T \ Kiselev took his place (PS 1.19.1917. Leo is a mortal threat to the nation in the same way, as that fourth block of the Chernobyl nuclear power station was constructed in the same time). The dates for the birth of the sole leaders of the republic coincide with the date of black for Belarus the Belarusian Republic. N. Slyunkov (04/26/1929), E. Sokolov (04/25/1926) The incident occurred during the 60th anniversary. This was the close of the orbital cycle. Both Taurus however, April was the only one was not looking positively for the country. Speaker of the Belarusian Parliament, N. Dementei (05/10/1931 Also Taurus) is not likely to differ from Belarus in the period of transition however, he will not cause anything wrong.

In the years following 1995 Belarus is likely to experience great luck and prosper, but it will only be a small amount of time.

In 1999, the future of Belarus as a state will be determined, because it is portion that is Lithuania (Cancer)

and Poland (Sagittarius as the private adversary and Poland (Sagittarius, the secret enemy Capricorn) and Poland (Sagittarius, the secret enemy of Capricorn) territorial disputes could be made. The republic will be threatened with dismemberment of Black Russia, Polesie, White Russia and Posozhie-Podneprovye, but this is likely to be avoided. Relationships with Lithuania (the one and only Capricorn adversary) following 2001 will strengthen relations, and will also improve social and political integration. Belarus is expecting a prolonged time of recovery.

Serious effects of the Chernobyl accident to Belarus can be attributed because it happened just following that the Sun was eclipsed by the Moon and is the control of Capricorn (a indication that is a sign of Belarus). Additionally, at the time of the disaster, Mars was in the constellation Capricorn and an eclipse of the sun can have the bloody, traumatic consequences. Thus, the majority of radioactive contamination is affecting the entire territory that is Belarus (Capricorn) as well as the northern part of Latvia as well as

Estonia (Capricorn), Finland (Capricorn), Sweden (Taurus) and Ukraine (Taurus) had less.

Are there more disasters to come? It's only the start, as all of humanity is experiencing an era of qualitative change. In 1994, there are going to occur a lot of accidents that involve electricity (nuclear power stations and hydroelectric power stations thermal power stations) This could cause electricity to cease serving the public which could cause short-circuits sparks of electricity, and spontaneous combustion. The man is reminded of the fact that technology is essential to search for alternative ways to develop. ,

Through 2008 Belarus will be an incredibly robust and tranquil state. The state will experience a handful of incidents, however they'll affect Belarus over a considerable period of time. Highly

The emotional backdrop will be heightened (due due to the effect from the moon) is likely to increase the emotional background, and a lot will determine the character and actions of

Saturn (ruler of Capricorn). This moment Saturn is located within the constellation Capricorn and this signals the start of the awakening of the national self-consciousness. If Saturn is in into the constellation Aquarius Other countries (for instance, Russia) will have spectacular successes, but there will be no success for Belarus. Belarus will not be among the richest. Russia will be significantly less affluent, Ukraine richer, and Russia will be a bit more prosperous for a while.

The region will be divided into a number of geographic zones (European Russia and Siberia, Europe's Russia and the Urals, Siberia, the Far East), so it is expected that they will join again after the process of integration begins but with a brand new spiritual foundation. Minsk is the capital of the Republic is associated with its zodiac star constellation Capricorn is always an artificial capital. Additionally, to from the southeast of Minsk there's an area that is a "difficult place", corresponding to the celestial star Capricorn in the sky.

Opulus.

Minsk is, just like Moscow is also a city with the ring-shaped structure, and it is divided into 12 areas, which correspond to the various significations of the zodiac. In accordance with the horoscopes of the city, which may be determined by the character of the relief, which is the place of rivers and subterranean sources, soils, and the climate. You can determine the local "places of power" and depressions or dips along with Nodal or energy-rich points. Indeed, the nature of those living in the city are largely determined by the year of birth and the current conditions.

Also that the horoscopes of cities (states) are constructed against the time.

* Howling Arrows and human horoscopes, oriented counterclockwise, to the direction of the Sun or the blood flowing through the body. The city's horoscopes are two in each that are conceived (from when the city was first thought of) as well as birth (when the first piece of land was pushed in during building process).

The fate of the other cities in Belarus: Gomel (the worst scenario, a very challenging fate, an enormous loss of life, desperation while Gomel was a city that was in a great location),

-- Brest-Litovsk (trade entrance to the republic, which will be filled with foreigners as well as the military), Grodno (modest, but a peaceful destiny), Lida (nothing special), Bobruisk (very *

intriguing city that has a very unpredictable fate, and Srazhanem

between extremes from one extreme to the next, natural catastrophes are probable from the year 1995), Baranavichy (a very complicated place, located on the iodine ray of Aries which is ruled by Mars and Mars. The Russian army was devastated there in 1916. It was then destroyed between 1994 and 1996. (or 199? year) in the wake of the conflict, the scenario can lead to bloody battles (# sh is a horrible and rare place the place where people from other countries will be), Pinsk (difficult fate), Orsha (incomprehensible place). In the other Belarusian city, it is expected that there may see changes, and an increasing decrease (people want to be the greener suburbs) In some areas (in particular, some industries) decline; and from these "good places" the force is likely to move elsewhere,

"DESTINIES OF RUSSIAN CITIES"

Moscow is not going to always remain the capital city of Russia. The city will likely shift towards Novgorod (the city located at Lake Ilmen), founded in the year 2000 by the zodiac signs of Aquarius that is unique to

We are independence, freedom and a lack of a rigid government. So why is it that *in Ancient Russia there were only Novgorod as well as Pskov were city republics. In them, the princes were only able to perform

to the wishes of the National Assembly. Petersburg (founded in Gemini, but in relief - Fish) was founded under Gemini however, as a relief area the constellation of Fish) isn't the ideal location for a capital city, as Pisces will do anything in order to "poison" Aquarius (Russia) with the life.

From Moscow that was an "good place" for a period of time, the force is gradually leaving, yet it is still an "holy city". The interactions between Moscow (Capricorn as per different sources - Taurus) as well as Russia (Aquarius) has been regarded as not to be a good thing and is filled by conflicts because of Capricorn's wish to rule Aquarius, Moscow, from the point at which it's likely to begin

People are leaving slowly, following 1994, they face difficulties, and problems with the underground and the karst cavity pose a risk, specifically in the south-west and north-west of the city. Above where the current capital city of Russia is situated. The near future could see there is a chance of catastrophe within one of the manufacturing facilities. Good places to be in - Sokolniki, Elk Island, South-West. From 1996 on, Moscow is expected to remain in position, though it might be able to withstand the shake-up. However, after 2001 Moscow is set to be revived however, it won't have its own meaning and over time, it's going to be unable to maintain its ring. The city is flourishing and an exciting future are in store for St. Petersburg (this center of European as well as Russian cultural activity will grow in popularity and the energy), Kiev (the spiritual renewal of which is challenging and was established around 1,500 years ago however, it was founded in between the second and third centuries BC) Rlsev (will be amazing and magnificent

City), Makaryev (trade city located in Kostroma region). Kostroma city in the Kostroma region).

"FUTURE OF THE REPUBLIC"

Ukraine. There is now a tense scenario. The early 1990s will bring different tensions, in the environmental and political realms, are potential. The country, which is connected to the constellation of Taurus and will be led by a Hetman selected to serve for 8 years (the time that is the period of Venus). Moldova is facing a difficult path and is at risk of being the third province in Romania, Lithuania (Cancer) is also experiencing a difficult time up to the time that most of the distant planets depart from the constellation of Capricorn at the end of 1991. However it is believed that the positioning of the planets can lead to the approval of its status as an independent nation.

Within Latvia (Virgo) it will be an advantage in comparison to other Baltic states. It will become a alliance of Latvians.

Latvia is awaiting the slow but extremely strong independence. Latvia will serve as the arbiter for settling disputes between Baltic nations following the disintegration of the Baltic Union, and subsequently conflict that have erupted between Russia as well as Poland. But 1991 is going to be a time of crisis. Potential disasters, particularly on the coastline. Kaliningrad is a region that could be affected by disasters, particularly along the coast. Kaliningrad region will be granted an exclusive status and become an "free territory" and will be a member of to the Baltic Economic

Community. Estonia (Capricorn) has been battling struggles with its ethnicity and financial problems. At the end of the century. a new Karelian-Finnish-Scandinavian ethnic group will emerge, which from the northwest will threaten Russia. The Far East, an accident like Chernobyl could occur in a nuclear-powered vessel sailing close to Vladivostok as well as in Khabarovsk between 1991 and 1992 there was bloody violence with grave effects could take place.

"WHAT ARE WAITING FOR COUNTRY OF SOCIALISM"

In Poland the country that is not going to be an economically prosperous country it is expected that a challenging time begins in 1994. In the meantime it is possible of an explosion in the shipyard. In Czechoslovakia between 1990 and

1995 would be an ideal time to start. If you're in the Czechoslovakian region, then there's a for example, OCQ.

Benno President V. Havel. Hungary Forecasts are generally positive, but during 1995-1997, a flood or earthquake could occur. Turkey is likely to experience an eruption of enthusiasm. By the close of the 90s, China will fall into multiple territories that will separate Tibet, Manchuria and Inner Mongolia. Massive social explosions are likely.

"FUTURE OF RUSSIA"

The Russian Astrologer V. Nemchin, who was alive in the 15th century recorded in his lifetime that "500 years later then, the rule of Satan would come into being. Temples would be demolished and sacred texts will be desecrated, and priests would be put to death within the earth. This will create a major risk to the dynasty that is ruling. The people will eat each other. 16 cities will fall and then reborn once more. " The prophet also predicted that by the 1980s in the 20th century "the northern population will receive three warnings regarding three" designated "(forbidden) methods must not be taken because if they do, for the next fifteen years, he'll suffer grave consequences. In for 15 years, nothing will be changed ",

The word"black" is repeatedly used in these three warnings. Since 1986, this prediction was to pass: 1986 Chernobyl The reserved pathway for science, nuclear power, that becomes the most terrifying Baal, devouring individuals.

1989 1989 Chernivtsi - - baldness in children as well as other horrible new illnesses because of thallium rainfall. "The "reserved" (forbidden) path is the one that has no intention to ensure health, but can disrupt the harmonious relationship between both nature and humankind which leads to genetic mutations that are not able to be stopped.

1988 1988 Karabakh ("Black hills" (in Turkic) The city falls under the aegis of Cancer National feuds as well as the division of territorial territories, bloodshed - the 3rd prohibited path that could cause people to fall into the pit of despair.

V. Nemchin also noted that "this satanic empire" will remain in existence as long as 3 evil elders remain in the system. this system of inhumanity, such as the death of of and the Koschey. As long as the last one of them dies then the system will continue to exist and if it doesn't, it's going to collapse. The three men ruling from the starting of Soviet power and endured for the longest time. Three of them:

V. Molotov (1890-1986, lived for 96 years);

G. Malenkov (1902-11988, lived for 86 years);

L. Kaganovich (born 11/22/1893, Sagittarius) is the third of three that remain living. At 97, he is the oldest and in the year 1986, he broke his thigh but was able to recover. The cold winter that lasted from 1990 to 1991 will be a disaster for him since the current system will fall apart. However, even if he regardless of his sins (for instance, the arranging of famines during the famine in Ukraine in 1933 and, after all, Sagittarius can be a symbol of Death for Taurus) and dies and dies, it is a tragedy. However, it is not possible to be destroyed, as blood shed will result in the only bloodshed and vengeance, just as it did in Romania. The man responsible for this was in the deliberative consent of Stalin transformed the thriving Ukraine to a desert and a proud population transformed into "zom'bi" (programmed dead) and brought with it not only physical but also spiritual hungry. Furthermore, the total of all the letters that make up the name, surname, and patronymics of Kaganovich (according to the ancient alphabet) is 666, which is the number for"the "apocalyptic beast".

Russia along with the rest of the world is currently in the middle of cosmic times. Nostradamus was a writer about this moment:

1989 1989 "There are great parades across the north,"

You can inquire about the conscience for this Yellow Serpent, Saturn and Jupiter end conflict,

A group of fifteen friends are gathered. "

"Parades" is the Big Parade of the Planets, that will run from 1982 until 1994. The year 1989 saw the appearance of"the" Yellow Snake, and the spiritual issues arose in a heightened way. Additionally, in the year the year 11989 there was a conflict with Saturn and Jupiter that was the result of a conflict of government and people. If the Allied Parliament hadn't been formed in 1989, all of the structures (the government and the other social institutions) would have been destroyed due to the fact that if seventy years (the precession cycle is a shift of the sky by one degree) in the years following its establishment the structure of the state doesn't evolve internally and eventually fall to pieces.

In the year 1990 (the Year of the Holy Spirit) the nation was stricken by disputes and social conflicts grew and aggravated

There was a rising focus on the spiritual world and to the religion and culture. The main focus is on the issue of spiritual renewal and rebirth, particularly in Ukraine. The economic challenges have risen significantly, in line with the combination with Saturn and Neptune within the constellation Capricorn.

The year 1991 is one of the most critical for the nation, as because of the escalating nature of the crisis as well as the paralysis in the government institutions of power, the mass activity is expected to increase.

1992-93: natural and social catastrophes. Massive earthquakes could occur (in particular, the Crimea). The likelihood of a coup d'état is low for it to occur. The military should be split with positive forces within it - not generals, who's interests and desires are well-known, but the representatives from the middle command (from Major to Colonel) that live in the same way than normal people. It is these forces that will help * to avoid a repetition of the October counter-revolutionary coup and bring the country out of the impasse, to which the "guiding and guiding force" led it. However, it won't happen soon, and the regime with the status of "civil consent" in 1991-1994 is likely to be a civil-military.

After an unending period of disorder and disease and distemper, our country will undergo an ebb and flow of development is set to begin on a distinct track. The "toys" of a technogenic society (weapons and computers.) are going to be used to a lesser degree. Between 1994 and 1996, the demise of the Soviet Union will definitely end in the 72-year period that will have passed since the creation of the USSR (12.20.1922) The Union was founded by the zodiac sign of Capricorn .. The Capricorn constellation is a part of the ideology of totalitarianism and brutally removing those unhappy to accomplish a specific objective. Capricorn has a bright outlook but in the meantime promotes a life of an asceticism.

The Soviet administration was created by the symbol of Scorpio that stings and eats up its citizens. An inhumane system can't be built on the basis of an idealistic idea. The one of Capricorn (USSR which is which is not by accident Moscow as well as Capricorn Capital) is set to achieve very high targets, but a rigid structure, which largely blocks people's individuality can be challenging to the population. . We always are surrounded by dead doctrines and phantom "socialist" values that were more important than the requirements of everyday people. And over the course of 76 years, the country was systematically isolated from global civilisation. One

But if the Bolsheviks. took 1 * power one month prior. when they tried to accomplish this in the month of July 1917. uninitiated with Libra initially, we'd have done better

stagnation, and a few people who were stagnation and a few. The system would become somewhat or not and many laws would be passed but there would be no follow-up. This job was substituted by a talk room. However, Soviet power was established in the month of November and our nation was able to embark on"Scorpion" path "Scorpion" path. The main element in every business is the beginning. .

"FORECAST FOR NEXT YEARS"

1990 (White Horse Year) 1990 was a fatal year (5 eclipses). Brain fermentation began There was a significant increase in suicides, heart attacks, insane. In this year, it's necessary to be a hard worker yet there is a strong temptation to organize, protest in an effort to accomplish all things effortlessly. In 1990's autumn an uncontrollable agitation of the masses and a rampant mafia. Between November and December, an unprecedented scene.

1991 (the year of the White Goat) - the most crucial year. The goat is an active animal and unpredictable happenings are expected in the coming year. Nobody knows what is to come. Unprofessional programs and sloppy officials are dangerous and can result in serious mistakes (in the finance sector, the industry and commerce). Political leaders must be vigilant prudent and responsible in the way they conduct themselves. This summer the martial law system is expected to be implemented across a variety of regions of the oppressive empire. The war against crime as well as mafia organizations will increase.

1992 (Black Monkey Year). The monkey is a dynamic, multi-faceted animal however, it is often doing "monkey work". This means that the year is likely to be interesting and exciting and productive, however not the most productive. 1993 (the year of the Blackish Rooster) - a significant risk of a coup, and the repression of democracy, and the freedom to speak. The rooster scours and displays that grain. They promise yet doing nothing. This year, deft and experienced politicians who claim peace, order and satisfaction are a risk.

1994 (Year of the Blue Dog) is the year that marks the beginning of an enjoyable life. The dog stays healthy however, he is worried often and barks during the late at night. There could be a variety of conflicts and inconsistencies. is trying to guard my Gobro.

1995 (Year of the Blue Pig) is an excellent year. However, you must not be waiting to see the year to come.

1996 (Year of the Red Rat) 1996 is the year of blanks and savings. It will also be the year of general growth. Television's global changes have begun following the resignation from M. Gorbachev.

The 90s will be a time when the spiritual, national and state awareness will be re-emerging all over the world, but specifically in our nation. The USSR is set to break up into several states as shown by the occurrence between Neptune and Uranus within the group of Mercury (1994) without meaning, looking forward to the political body. 1994 is the year that will see the establishment of new capitals and new areas of free zone and territory (Petersburg, Vyborg, Novgorod, Sakhalin, Primorsky Krai). The year 1994 marks the conclusion of the Parade of Planets, when the chaos and troubles have a tendency to diminish as the conditions in Russia will get back to normal. There is a chance that Russia is likely to be broken up into many smaller state-owned entities that are linked to the structure of border with some new connection. Then, at the close of the

1990s, and in the early years into the 20th century an interim separation of the various populations will take place, in order that all of them can be able to recognize their own integrity (it's not by accident that we are going back to its roots of its culture, and is reviving the national traditions) as well as its role in the world Earth and the necessity to join with people from other nations and at a more advanced scale.

1996: A new president of Russia will be in power in 1996, under the zodiac signs of Aquarius and will succeed M. Gorbachev, but within a specific amount of time. Based on his personality and abilities, he'll look like Peter I. However, he will have an position is opposite to Peter (Peter who was the greatest "cut a window into Europe" and ruthlessly destroyed ancient customs and traditions). The leader who will be elected to the nation, mighty and bright, will take the course of renewal of the primitively Slavic and, in contrast to Peter is the "bright man" and the blood of his fellow citizens won't be shed. He is expected to rule for only seven years (119 percent -- 2003) however, he is expected to perform a great job. But, prior to his rule it is possible to be in danger to "victory, in Russia a narrowly nationalistic or ecclesiastical trend, which is now reborn rapidly, being a blessing for the people only from one side."

1994-1996: The first Uygehi economics after the triple connection that was the result of Uranus and Neptune within the constellation of Capricorn. There is a sense that the majority of people within Russia is expected to bow to the $-nyat monarchy. Naturally the traditions of monarchy within Russia are extremely solid, but they will not be the monarchy is a good thing, neither. the rule of law and no republican system, nor any other type of social structure that existed before in Earth within Russia eventually. When 1996 comes around, Uranus moves into the sign of Aquarius and a new era will be ushered in to the nation that will be a time of absolute peace, and a total change occurs in the governance of the nation. It will create a new structure with no precedent to the past history of the Earth in the next decade, and by 2003 the establishment of the new structure will be completed. The entire time of preparing for the new phase, which is the slow process of aligning the world is expected to end in 2003.

#

1996-2003 Russia (the nation of Aquarius) changes faster than other countries and is likely to undergo one of the most profound and drastic transformations, also known as "shock therapy." Following political instability and a resurgence of ecological crises, and the increase of man-made catastrophes are feasible. Since 2003, there has been a spiritual take-off has been a true growth of every spirituality with steady growth, you can be in the same place within the world that we do today we are japanese. The characteristics that characterize the Russian population as a love of creativity, innovation and creativity during the Aquarian period will be particularly useful .. They are able to swiftly switch careers, be open to the latest trends, and completely alter their thinking and not be a slave to old-fashioned practices. Within the borders of the ex- USSR there is a chance that the issue of nationalists will disappear completely. The year 2000 could bring disasters within southern Russia. In 2010 it is predicted that the Black Sea will catch fire because of hydrogen sulfide that is being released from below and reaching the sea's surface.

Chapter 5: The World Of The Future

2000 is a new era will be beginning in the human history with no parallels prior to. The year 2003 marks the start of the period of Great Lady's reign, as it is the Aquarian time, in contrast to the Pisces male-dominated era women will have a major part .. The women are among the most subtle of entities and they'll be the carriers of our civilization . In any time period, but especially at. an era of change, and incur an influx of.-ideas. TSIVI- *.

lizatsii, poskrlku. they. using: lkrbyh situations. ^ {through,

The antennas of plants) remain in contact to the Cosmos. At the end of the century. is the beginning of an entirely new matriarchy. There will be many Great Dame, including in Russia and located in the East.

When the time of one of these ladies, there is the possibility of a fresh Great Flood. Nostradamus predicted that by 2032, some areas in England, Holland, Denmark, Finland, coastal areas from other countries will gradually become flooded, which will last until 2050-2060. and then it will begin to slow. The time of women's control is expected to last until 2003, after which it will be a period of 2104 and beyond.

As of 2023, as per Nostradamus In 2023, according to Nostradamus, the Earth could be lowered off its orbit. Around the turn of the century, Nostradamus, the great astrologer as well as the clairvoyant was a writer:

"The forthcoming parade of the XXI century Europe as well as the Temple will be separated and The Two Suns live and black are coming from the South. The stars' saints guide the people. "

The world will see the division of individuals, according to their personal worldview and their inner world, in "higher" and "lower" '(monkey-like). The higher (inspired) individuals will sport stunning faces, gorgeous hair, and beautiful skin. Part of the new

the human race as a result contact with aliens will develop incredible capabilities.

In the Northern Hemisphere (Russia, the Middle East, India, -- China) it will see the "golden age". The countries of these regions will become an area of goodness for the entire world. The justice kingdom starts from the borders of our nation ("the second peak of Saturn").

Nostradamus predicted that between 1994 and 1996 in the region of Yad-Ran

(Adriatic Sea) In the Adriatic Sea between 1994 and 1996 "a marvelous fish with a human head" could be taken. In 1998, the threat that would lead to an 3rd World War would arise However, it is possible to be averted, however at the beginning in the XXI century a war of energy on the consciousness level may be possible. The idea of the English language in 2012 will be weakened as the European idea of civilization could be replaced by other ideas.

In the early XXI century, an enormous ethnic impact from the black race is expected to be observed. Nostradamus recorded this in his writings:

"Black devils in Africa are quiet, What is now living gloomily in oblivion, Ascending to the throne in this world is faceless, After 500 years there will be the first salute."

However, these fellows will be inspirated by communist ideologies that have already become a part of history for the majority of us. These "black devils" will take control of the West by capturing America, Western Europe, Africa as well as a part of South Asia. The next step (in 2005 and 2012) will be the division in the United States, its disintegration and demise. America. United States (R. Nehru: "In a country on the other side of the ocean, leaders have four years to govern. The final number is 44." (J. Bu" n" - just 41 of them presidents from the United States.) A little time left. The next question is: There is a risk of a complete triumph of the concept of communism across America, Africa, Western Europe. Imagine, for instance, the collective farm of Texas or a competition for social status with Paris and London or The Challenge of the Red Banner of European

nations.   Minnesota's   workforce
Minnesota were greeted by a delegation
from The Communist Party of Italy. It's
terrible! It's a disaster! the XXI and the
start of the XXII century, in the words of
Nostradamus, "Western Europe will be
overrun by the race of yellow (Asians).
There will be many and very well-armed
",

* In our nation (in Russia, China and the
other "good countries") it is going to be
totally different and in the years
following 2003, there will never be any
gulags, nor massive unannounced
populations. There will however be an
end to the C1rash forces, which are still
in power within us. It's not a coincidence
that, in the 20th century the satanic
forces were defeated in the East and
where "God prepared a dungeon for
them."

Understanding cosmic laws as well as the pursuit in inner harmony for mankind is crucial for those in the early XXI century. That is, the time at the time that SATANA arrives on Earth and will be granted enormous power and immense strength and show up before the humanity by the name of the ANTICHRIST.

The Antichrist is expected to be born in 1999. The Antichrist will be able to reach the entire world to be recognized by the end of 2020s. His coming will be announced throughout the 2000s and into 2005, numerous fake prophets will be seen while false prophets be broadcasting about some sort of supernatural religion.

The coming of the Antichrist will be more terrifying than that of the legend of "apocalyptic beast" with the number 666. Antichrist is likely to charm a lot of people, particularly the simple and true West. This will be an utterly terrible lying liar because lying is a tool to bring about Evil. It is this person that, with the aid of an alchemical elixir that is based upon tellurium, will attain immortality. The condition will stay the same over the course of time, so it's very difficult to take on his. "

Satan might die, however Satan will reincarnate in the form of the brand new Savior in this World, Jesus Christ, following the teachings of the *wah. In fact, two millennia ago, Christ took on the entire world to atone for his sins. He took his own life as the ultimate sacrifice. Today, the Antichrist will use demagogy, tries to cause humanity to suffer and suffer while insisting that it's a wonderful benefit.

This is the thing that the true Antichrist is about, as it is described in the "Revelation of John the Theologian"; "And the dragon gave him his strength and his throne and great power ... And the deadly cancer of this zvgerya will be healed ... And who can fight with him! .. And he opened his mouth to blaspheme against God, and power was given to him over every nation and power to act 42 months. "

After that, the Antichrist (Satan) --the real creature of the World will appear with the appearance of human form, you will be referred to as the second Christ (Nomacanic God), the son of Man and the third Savior (the first was Zaratuetra and the second the name was Yeshua (Jesus) Nodri). He'll rule in a joyful phase of spiritual regeneration and will introduce people to in the New Testament - a new perspective on the world, a message which will bring people together and aid in the separation of those who are light from those who are dark. This teaching will focused on the region of Russia as well as Western Siberia.

He'll appear all over the world at once as lightning. This is in the Gospel of Matthew (ch. 24, pp. 27-30): "As lightning descends from the East and can be observed all the way to West and West, the same will be arrive the un-human Son ... The sun will dim and the Moon does not shed its lights and the stars will disappear from the the IE (? an, and the powers that govern the sky will be shaken ... The event will take place in winter months and on Saturdays. The text explains the lunar and solar eclipses occurring in close proximity to one another however, they typically are not in sync. Lightning is a symbol of Uray which is who is the ruler of Aquarius which begins in 2003 as well as the complete solar eclipse, according to the text is scheduled to occur close to the solar system Uranus. If you reduce the area of your search, you will be able to find the date of birth of Jesus Christ, the Son of Man - February 5, 2000. Also, unidentified comets in the shape of a crown has been seen before close to the Earth during the 6th century BC and will pass through the location of his birth (in the Volga basin). It was at exactly the time that Jesus Christ was born. Jesus Christ and led the Persian people of the Volor-Zoroastrians back to Palestine to worship the newly-born Savior in the World. Nostradamus was a writer about the birth of Jesus Christ: "Although the planet Mars is situated before the conclusion of its rotation, all things will begin with the start. Numerous planets will be grouped in the constellation Aquarius and some will go dark for a long time. Resurrected and reborn Christ will be revealed as well as Bliss is expected to arrive so that Evil has to stay within its craters for an extended period of time. "

2. CHRIST is expected to be recognized by all the world around 2032-2033 (when it's the age of 33) and at the time, a massive comet is about to be passing again near Earth. The ruler will be crowned of Russia at the beginning in 2033. He'll rule the country for 1 every space-day (72 Earth-years) and bring the very best to Russia. Discontented Russia could become the home for the revival of religion in this Christian world.

Numerous astrologers also drew attention to another Nostradamus Quatrain that is like the "second coming of Christ," and describing it as an indication for the 3rd World War or a nest for the Mongol King, also known as the New Genghis Khan who, according to them, will sweep out all the civilizations.

This verse sounds like:

The year 1999 is in the seventh month "A huge and terrible ruler will come down from the heavens,

for the rebirth of the great Angol-mua King. This will be a difficult battle.

However, he'll rule with joy in the days before and even after Mars. "

"Angol-mua" - in French is "angelic month" (time from Easter until Ascension) in which Christ was resurrected. Christ in the mythology, was one of one of his followers. The quatrain also signifies that the six-month appearance of the Christ who is now Jesus Christ who is the Savior of the world. The word "ANGOL" a conscious mistake was committed, as Nostradamus codified every quatrain using an numerological code (according that a particular numeral corresponds to every letter) to ensure that the sum of all the number of digits in the final is a figure which is the key to an exact year.

Also, in 1999, a singular cosmic event is expected to occur: one of the largest eclipses to occur on Sun on August 8th, 1999 (29.07 per the Julian calendar, which is the "7th month"), in which the planets of the Solar System will be located as the cross. Mars and Saturn meet. To the West Astrologers see the cross to be a symbol of war in the world, devastating happenings and changes. This is actually an imminent birth for the great king and the credo of the "bright man." It happened to planets in the year of Alexander's birth. Alexander the Great.

The possibility of a major war exists in the event that planets don't face each other but gather (like clouds prior to a storm) within a particular region of sky. As an instance that the 1st World War and the 2nd World Wars began when all planets were gathered together within the constellations of Aries up to Cancer.

The modern Christ as well as the Antichrist be prefigured by their predecessors. One of them is dark magician A. Kashpirovsky (born August 11, 1939. 60 years prior to the momentous event! 1.08.1999, i.e. for the entire Eastern cycle "rajan" (eastern century). He

The man was discovered 11 years prior to the emergence of Antichrist and the appearance of him was not by chance. In carrying the response to the event, Cosmos as it checks the reactions of individuals to the future. Kashpirovsky could wish others to be well however, as a psychotherapist who is psychic, he is a black-field therapist, which means that the therapist is not sure of the exact nature of what he's doing. He, however, being an extremely proud and arrogant person, believed that was a prophet, an eminent saint, and a powerful healer. God is not to blame him if he chooses the route of Evil as Kashpirovsky is a hugely responsible person, not just for himself. In the end, if the influence he exerts on everyone and cause an epidemic of insanity.

It is generally believed that by the conclusion of 1990, an untrue prophet will be revealed in Russia after which will come the false prophet. They are servants of the Antichrist, and his coming will occur at the beginning of the 21st century.

2035-2050 - The 1st "cosmic battle between Christ and the Antichrist, a clash of the forces of Light, led by the Savior of the World and the forces of Darkness, will take place, and the forces of Goodness and Light will triumph. And after this event, mankind will learn to manage time." : "And the Son of Man was seen by Satan, he took the dragon, the ancient serpent, who is the Devil and Satan, and brought him to the bottomless pit, and put him in prison, so that he would not deceive the nations, forging for 1000 years" (Revelation of John Theologian, Chapter 20).

"GREAT THRESHOLD"

Beginning at beginning in 199! This year starting from 199! year, Russia (the nation in Aquarius) the time that is known as the Great Everlasting and chaos will be upon us, making it impossible to believe in the best or even an overseas uncle. Additionally, Western countries with an economic system that is not developed, and in which they live in relative peace and are currently in the middle of a revolution and are on the brink of collapsing, since there will be a time which will force everyone to develop their talents as well as developed nations do not have the capacity to protect either technology or lkpa, as there will be a search for the valuable insignificant ys-by-nowhere. Then, the natural world will end up being destroyed.

Humanity will be challenged qualitatively because of the crisis that is looming, and lastly all, every person is born to ignite a fire of God within him, and to expose the principles of harmony and joy.

People who reside blissfully in the West with their illusory utopia but at the same time are deprived of the benefits of civilisation ("toys" which distract people from their own development) to live in an era of crisis. In the 21st century, countries that have adapted to living in harsh environments are better prepared and in the next changes to the global circumstances, it'll be much easier to the rest of us (the "torn off child of civilization") to live and to change, as our culture is not accustomed to living a life of luxury. When the crisis begins to erupt within the West there is a high probability that it will be difficult for them to stay out of an overall decline.

Then we (the civilisation of Aquarius) have finally arrived at the point of after shedding the falsehoods we were given for the past 70 years, can begin living an ordinary life and develop our capacities and opportunities inherent in our human nature. We will not be going on the road of growth of statehood but rather the pathway of developing the spiritual principles, in harmony with the natural world. In addition, we have immunity against all massive lies. Now, it's hard to convince the people of our country, there is a lot to doubt about the myth of a wise grandfather, unless real proof can be presented. In the West this kind of immunity, which is foremost spiritual but not so much so, and the population there is highly insecure. Then they won't have the time to eliminate tempting illusions. However, they'll be too late. Then, they will start the exams that we've already cleared.

"WHO SURVIVES"

When 1996 comes around, and Uranus is in into the constellation Aquarius the nature "will rise against man." From 1996 to 2003 and perhaps from the beginning of the XXI century huge catastrophic cataclysms and catastrophes as well as worldwide climate shifts will be in full swing. Earthquakes, storms, turbulent geochemical processes, cooling flooding, droughts, epidemics with endless rains and raging wind will strike the everyone. At the edge of historic times, some of the most extraordinary and unpredictable of events are set to occur.

Many changes are anticipated throughout the solar system due to the fact that (according according to Nostradamus) the "descendants will be spared the opportunity to observe all the planets" they are in view. The moon's influence is affecting our planet, will cease at the end of 2000 "many stars will approach the Earth at a dangerous distance and cause global cataclysms, especially in climate."

However, it is only humankind's preparation for the global changes. A lot of people are unaware of the passing of time and also, previously undiscovered magical, supernatural powers that are typical for every individual (clairvoyance and the ability to shift between the space-time continuum, psychic ability healing, telekinesis, and levitation) are resurfacing within their bodies. As we enter the age of cataclysms within us all the species' protection is awakened the abilities that were laid in us by our nature.

It's like having a vision of a global disaster as well as the potential for death. The limitless capabilities that can help someone be able to survive. However as per experts' predictions 1 to

3/3-2 / three of the human race could die in the process of transitioning the Earth into a new form. The people will be forced to return to the activities they previously feared but had not. This is the only way to get back the foundations to our growth and self-knowledge. It is not possible to live better or more, we will just live differently.

The future generation will be focused on the growth of human characteristics that are new and for them it's a continuing life and the beginning of a new and exciting life. The process is expected to begin at the beginning of the 21st century, and last for as long as 2 000 years. The assumption is that the development of a new breed of occultists is based on the genetics of Ukrainian and Belarusian peoples. In both cases, the catastrophe of Chernobyl was a major factor as an increase in background radiation causes rapid growth of genetic mutations and increasing numbers of individuals will develop peculiar abilities, and have unique mechanisms of protection for themselves. It is vital to be aware of these powers in order to be able to recognize them, or else one cannot relax, and attain spiritual tranquility. The people born January 1!! February 19 and April 7! May 30, July 30 September 117, the 5th of November, will feel this extraordinary ability.

The new generation of people, who are made up of people born from a new generation who adjust to the changing circumstances of life on Earth and are genetically more robust. Others who are unable to discover these talents within themselves, and aren't conscious of their purpose they will be unable to grasp the greater principles of the Cosmos and cannot endure the changing conditions (including submerged and underwater) and even try to stay out of the pitfalls of modern technology. Then they'll be destroyed and swept away like fragments of ice in a swirl. In the current form that it is in and grows, its end will be inevitable. What is in fact, that impedes the process of evolution, which is the growth of consciousness and the mind of both man and nature is a violation of harmony in the world, and is not sustainable. The 21st century is a time when those who are at odds with the rules of Cosmos will be greeted by massive changes (over 10-15 generations) as well as painful, slow loss of health.

>> "The boundaries of Heaven and Earth will expand, and they will be one." The world is beginning to realize the connection between the cosmic sphere, which is where our ancestors' distant

past were from. Technology will enable us rise to the next level of progress while the spirit and thoughts that are located within Space and the Universe, will be an even more powerful force in the transformation of material and creativity of our world. Only those who discover the hidden energy reservoirs within man, and who understand that the most important law in Cosmos can be described as the principle of evolutionary development, that impressed I. Kant. German philosopher I. Kant, and that he observed in every human being, are able to live their lives with harmony.

This is, in essence, an ethical and moral law in that Evil at any level can be considered a breach of harmony. It is a law system that is universal in its scope. The knowledge they have of those that use them to harm others, enables people to control the minds of other people. It is

by far the most dangerous weapon because when you know the horoscope of an individual and their physical appearance, you are able to pick the time when someone feels the most secure and calm. There is no have to be removed as he is constantly in the midst of a thought which eventually will be his own thoughts. The mind is able to be manipulated and compelled by others to perform the actions they require. Ray-sh EUR dollar guarantee to ensure to prevent this from happening is knowing the things you require as well as what you don't but nothing can harm your or ruin it !. Only then will you start to understand clearly. Most people will be living underground, in bunkers. They are hopeless mutants "orange people **
According to Nostradamus, by the middle of the XXI century, humankind on Earth

will be divided into 3 races:" Bright (Europeans as well as Asians),

"Dark" (people of evil)"Dark" (people of evil) "orange" (degenerates). "Orange" people will rise between the realm of Light and Darkness. They'll cut se'bya off of existence and create a cycle of existence. They will end up dying, turning into

Chapter 6: Life And Times Of The Prophet

Historian ...

Inform our children about our unfortunate fate

To read, and grieve for our demise,

Let them let their parents' sins remind them of their fathers.

The same fates that brought misfortunes to others could happen to you.

Ronsard, Discours des miseres de ce temps

It's not enough to contemplate the writings of Nostradamus in the sense that they represent an oracle that is originating outside the normal boundaries of time and space. Nostradamus was a real person who was flawed as every human being. He was also the historical figure. His way of speaking as well as the specific events on the subject he pondered, and the way in which he thought were affected by the era in which he was born. If we want to get near to comprehending the ideas or all of Nostradamus or perhaps discover the causes that we aren't able to comprehend We must know what happened to the world which produced him.

It is commonplace to think of the present as a dangerous time that is characterized by the risk of destruction by mass by a multitude of means. There is no doubt that we've got the power to completely destroy ourselves as a species and even take the world with us. In the modern globe, most people often, feel comfortable and protected. However, the terrible events of the present should be a topic for open and global discussion.

Media, democracy and the internet give us the sense of having the impression of being able to direct our lives, and at a minimum, some impact on how events unfold. This is where the gap that we have with the common French person or woman from the 16th century couldn't be greater.

France in the Sixteenth Century

The time was when France was not even a country. Aquitaine and Provence have only joined during the preceding century. there was still a dispute about Calais as well as other areas which were claimed from Calais and other territories claimed by the Holy Roman Emperor, and Brittany was not united up to 1547. Local lords had a lot of influence and the local customs held influence, which meant that laws of the monarchy were frequently useless. The rights and position of peasants varied however they generally weighed very tiny - most aristocrats would value their horses more than an entire village of peasants. Communication was virtually nonexistent since there was not a postal system with only an inefficient and costly network of couriers. The roads were for the majority, dirt roads and were only accessible by horseback and not in any horse-drawn carriages. The daily life of a common human being was painful, difficult and generally short. On the other hand, the lives of the aristocratic had some advantages however they faced the constant threat of dying through intrigue in the hands of the aristocracy's peer group.

The powerful rulers like Henri II and his wife Catherine de' Medici strove to unite the struggling kingdom, however they faced greater than just internal discord.

The time was the final Renaissance which was when the spirit of humanity exploded through the likes of Michelangelo, Erasmus, Rabelais, Raphael and Leonardo da Vinci. Magellan tried to navigate across the globe and scientific research was progressing and the aristocracy was creating breathtaking scenes like the famous reunion with Henry VIII and Francis I in the Field of the Cloth of Gold. The plague, however, was widespread and transformed entire towns into open graves. Europe was continually frightened with The Ottoman Turks whose barbaric cruelty and obsession with conquest dominated with the current European brain. Robbers also racked up throughout the landscape. The wars of religion would take over 150,000 French individuals before the closing century. It was also a time that was ruled by Calvin and Luther and the new

Protestantism had begun to fight the powerful forces of the Inquisition as well as the Jesuits. If that weren't enough it got worse in the middle of the century, to cause agricultural crisis and massive famine. The formidable king Henri II, would allow himself to be executed during a duel, in spite of the advice of Nostradamus. soldiers from armies that were disbanded and robbers joined in killing and pillaging, the children from Henri and Catherine had a chance to be crowned and perish, and hate affected everyone in the throne, from the top to the lowest levels, when Protestant and Catholic leaders plotted against another. Nostradamus was born in a time in which the Apocalypse appeared imminent and that the Four Horsemen, plague, the famine, war and even death searched the country.

The Early Life of Michel de Notredame

Michel de Notredame (or Nostredame) was born around noon on the 14th of December 1503 in St-Remy-de-Provence. There was a discrepancy with respect to both the Julian calendar and the Gregorian calendar and the Sun is believed to enter Capricorn on around the Winter Solstice on or around December 22 at present it was at the 2nd degree of the Cardinal earth sign when he was born. birth. He was born conjunct (Le. set within the zodiac) as well as Mercury as well as Midheaven. Midheaven Astrologers consider to be a perfect match for someone who would later achieve fame through his words. The horoscope for Nostradamus that was drawn on his birthday at Salon It is available to provide interest. It should however be pointed out that no real or authentic chart of the seer is available It is also one of the many mysteries surrounding the existence of Nostradamus which is that, during the days when horoscopes had been frequently drawn to predict births, no chart was likely to be drawn specifically for Nostradamus.

He was the son of a successful merchant named Iaume de Notredame. He was the child of the Jewish merchant named Guy Gassonet. Guy changed his religion to Christianity at the age of 1463. He adopted his surname Pierre to honor the local bishop, and de Notredame in honor of his participation in the Visitation of our Lady during the time that the transformation was celebrated. It is believed that the family was a part of people from the Spanish Jews who had fled persecution over the past two centuries. Michel's maternal grandfather was the one who took care of his schooling, teaching the young man in

Latin as well as Greek as well as the sciences of astrology, astronomy, medicine as well as chemistry, herbal medicine and possibly maths. Michel was said to have an uncontrollable humorous sense of humor as well as a passion for learning as well as an appreciation for the classical literature. When he was 16 He enrolled in the college of Avignon to study language, rhetoric and logic as well as to be popular for his quick and sharp wit. His name, which was prophetically called him the tiny Astrologue. But the college was broken up in 1520, when the plague began to spread eastward.

In the years that followed, Michel was the wandering Jew moving between places collecting knowledge of herbal remedies and medicinal plants, and their roots. The nation was in a state of flux as it was under threat from the Turks as well as in the Holy Roman Empire and by disease, and Nostradamus was able to treat those sick and collecting invaluable experience. At the age of 25 young, Michel enrolled for his doctorate at the Montpellier medical school, which was possibly funded by the money of his father. The legend says that he was admitted to the faculty following the obtaining of the doctorate. However, there are no records of that however, whatever the circumstances it was not long before he began again on his journey and later set up as a physician in Agen fifteen years later, around 1533. He met there one man who's Latinised title as Julius Caesar Scaliger, a authentic Renaissance personality, proficient in the sciences, arts and the grammar and soon they were acquaintances. Michel was also said to have married the woman of great beauty He settled in the area and had two sons.

The Nostradamus horoscope.

A tragedy struck and Michel's entire family was struck off by the plague. Michel's reputation wasn't helped due to his inability to protect his family members and also his deceased spouse's family filed a lawsuit against him, probably to get back the dowry she received. According to reports, he was also summoned before the Inquisition for some comments made in relation to the creation sculptures depicting the Holy Virgin that sounded like potential Protestant sentiments. Scaliger did not agree with the Inquisition, as he's been doing with the majority of people. Perhaps depressed and sad,

Michel de Notredame began for another journey. He was returning to Provence and tended to patients who were plagued in Marseille after which in 1546, he was taken to Aix-en-Provence in the same capacity as well as to Salon. His fame as a plague doctor was gaining momentum and there are accounts of how his patients were swarmed with gifts that were donated to charity (possibly due to the fact that they were difficult to carry). In Salon the doctor met his second wife, newly widowed, well-off Anne Ponsarde, but they were not able to settle down as they were summoned for an epidemic in Lyon which shook the city. The citizens cried"We are looking for to be the hero of Aix I'm sure he may be able to be able to save Lyon like he did Aix.

11 November 1547, aged of 43 Michel de Notredame was became the wealthy widow. They bought a well-known residence in Salon. But he didn't reside there at the time, preferring instead to travel to Italy. The reason for this trip

could have been different than previous trips, since Nostradamus was attracted to areas like Florence where manuscripts from the past were translated by Renaissance experts. The evidence suggests that Nostradamus wanted to further develop his skills in prophecy studying the writings of esotericists like Marsilio Ficino, and his student, Pico della Mirandola. There were translations available for Pythagoras, Plato, Hermes Trismegistos as well as of a variety of magical texts, including the infamous Clavicula Salotnonis or Key of Solomon, supposedly handed down by Solomon, the Biblical King himself. It contained guidelines for theurgy i.e. calling in spirits as well as gods and demi-gods. To seek out arcane or occult knowledge, and possibly trying to improve his genetic psychic talents, Nostradamus also visited Naples, Palermo and possibly Sicily.

Nostradamus the Seer

The people of our time who want to improve their intuition are attracted to nature that frees our intuition by pointing to old monuments that are suffused with wisdom from the past, as well as to books and similar minds, which can help you discover ideas that stimulate and show the mysteries. There is a good chance that Nostradamus was able to find all of the sources of inspiration during his trips. After three years of travel in the year 47 Michel de Notredame came back to his home in Salon with his new spouse and the best period of his life.

This was when the first time he began signing his name 'Nostradarnus', and then to release his Almanachs. These were booklets that predicted the weather with a bare-bones terms of content. They were glorified forecasts for weather predictions and a few remarks on issues of military and politics. As we've witnessed, conditions of the weather were a huge concern during the sixteenth century of France as a large number of people lost their lives due to an insufficient harvest during the Little Ice Age. The Almanachs proved to be a hit, and brought the Almanachs fame and fortune and also some recognition as prophet.

Nostradarnus in his capacity as a physician was ahead of his time realizing the benefits of fresh air as well as clean, running water in preventing and treating plague. In this regard, he devoted both time and money into the creation of an intricate network of canals surrounding Salon. Additionally, guided by the signs and omens, He began to work on what would be the most significant success of his existence and that is the reason why we recognize him: his prophecies that were designed to predict the future of the globe. Utilizing his mind, the wealth of his experience, and education, he got to work, writing his prophecies as quatrains or verses with four lines. He wanted to write 10 volumes made up from 100 quatrains. every volume was referred to as centurie. It is possible to misunderstand the meaning of this term as it had nothing to be concerned with the 100-year period however, when you consider the nature of prophecies it's a reasonable oversight.

The years came to be alongside the first of Anne and Nostradamus"children" and, by the mid-point of 1554, he had completed his centurion. Thanks to his contacts in the fields of philosophy and literature It was easy to have his work published and his first collection of 353 lines was put out into the world in the spring of 1555.

The fame was immediate, and resulted in a royal summons issued by the Queen Catherine de' Medici and in July, the prophet had been riding uncomfortably toward Paris with saddle sores and even thinking about the possibility of a grisly end was in store for him during the night of intrigue that was a part of the magnificence of court. The moment he reached in Paris before he was summoned to the Queen's throne for a an audience in private and later seated in luxurious quarters, in which he conducted a number of lucrative meetings - and was in the process of being afflicted with severe gout because of the high standard of life! A look at the constitutions and horoscopes for three princes made his drained and one of the most effective things way to address the

Queen was "all your sons will reign as the kings'. The Queen did not seem to be aware of the gloominess in the remark, and could no doubt have kept him in the court along with other occultists with whom she was connected. The Parisian authorities had started to look into the practices of the occult. Nostradamus who was able to avoid the Inquisition at least once on a earlier occasion, decided discretion was the best part of bravery and departed Paris immediately.

The interim version of the Propheties was published after the devastating military catastrophe of St-Quentln on August 15, 1557. The Spaniards caused massive losses, bringing darkness and doom over the entire nation. The autumn of 1557 was the year, a fourth child Andre was born to Nostradamus and his wife. Their oldest child, Madeleine, was now at the age of six.

Cesar the one who would be his father's most famous exponent was only three, while Charles was the youngest. At a time when the age of 55 was considered to be an old age, the pressures of one's young family on an older prophet would have sounded overwhelming, yet all of the one thousand quatrains were complete by June 1558. But, in the course of this year the world was shaken by many turmoils, as well as some very brutal attacks against Nostradamus himself. The tract, written in Latin was titled The Premiere Invective of Seigneur Hercules the Prancois against Monstradamus in which Hercules explained the astrology of Nostradamus as an immoral attempt to pull God off the horizon with his beard', and replace him with without any real meaning. Insane personal abuse followed and was accompanied by the claim that his reliance on Astrology was sorcery fooling those who read it. (Source: Laurent Vidal Declaration des Abus Ignorances et Seditions de Michel Nostradamus, 1558.) A different pamphlet that is likely taken from the same source, was titled Le Monstre d'Abus, which is a homophonic adverb of Nostradamus' name, looking like a copy of the methods that were used in the Green Language, used by the prophet (see chapter 2 to learn further details about the Green Language). Personal and venomous attacks like this were commonplace during the period, yet could not have been a great way to help the prophet. It is unclear if this was due to a dispute among editors, it is believed that some passages were lost in this time however it was not until two years following the death of the seer in 1568, that a entire work was published however, there were 58 verses in the 7th century had been left out. The lost verses are still missing to this the present.

By Royal Appointment

The publishing issues aside however, the country was in turmoil due to the tragic loss of the King Henri II, who was playing. Henri was a tough and brave, but indiscreet, monarch who was able to hold together the belligerent and ramshackle provincial system that was in place during the Sixteenth century of France. Then disaster struck with it, and a period of 50 years conflict and turmoil were set to ensue. The demise of Henri was reportedly predicted as well by the Italian Astrologer Luca Gaurica, who had advised the King to stay clear of all single-fighting inside a sealed space' particularly during the forty-first year' and by the prophet Nostradamus. Absolutely Queen Catherine as well as her court believed that Henri's passing of the king was an indication of the century I quatrain of XXXV.

Le lyon ieune le vieux surmontera

En champ bellique par singulier duelle

Dans caige d'or les yeaux luy creuera:

Deux classes une, puis mourir, mort cruel.

The lion's young will take on the older,

on a battlefield that is warlike, when fighting in a single battle.

A gold-plated cage the man will be able to pierce the eyes of his victim:

Two wounds are one of them. He is then slain by a brutal death.

The Quatrain of this quatrain has essentially created famous the name of Nostradamus. Even despite all cautions that the King insisted on playing against the Captain of his Scottish Guardsmen, Montgomery. Montgomery was hesitant, as he was significantly younger than the King, however there was no chance of getting around the royal challenge. Both were jousting in the 3rd day contest held at St Antoine that marked the wedding of the daughter of Henri's, Elisabeth married to the King Philip from Spain (erstwhile wife of unhappy Mary Tudor) and Henri's sister Marguerite to the Due de Savoie. Both King as well as Montgomery were lions in their coats of arms. In the third fight, Montgomery's lance penetrated the helmet gilded by the King (dans caige or...) which penetrated his brain and face near the top of his eye. There were also wounds in the throat. Ten days later he died in agony.

The event, though devastating for France however, helped to increase the reputation and trustworthiness of the sage. Nostradamus continued his work with Almanachs and also with less well-known pieces on treating the symptoms of plague as well as about the astrology. Also, he was consulted by powerful nobles on the future as well as their own fortune. The canons of Orange even contacted him. Canons from Orange concerning the location of their treasures stolen. But in the age of war and fear those like Nostradamus weren't always secure. Witchcraft accusations were always a possibility. Also, due to his Jewish origin and was generally considered to be 'different in his beliefs, he was not suspected as a Protestant. In addition, there was the risk of angering the most prestigious client and you can wonder about the possibility that

Nostradamus was spared torture and met with the wrath of his enemies. Perhaps the support of Queen Elizabeth II, widowed The shrewd and naive Catherine de' Medici, might have saved Nostradamus. He began to build his Sixains and on the day that they completed them in the month of October, 1564 Catherine de' Medici arrived at Salon together with her 14-year-old son the Charles IX. Charles IX. The family of the royals had come to meet their seer on their two-year trip designed to unify the nation in turmoil as well as arthritis-stricken Nostradamus was enlisted to deliver publicly the greeting address.

In this particular event, Henri, Prince de Beam was also there and it is believed that it was at this point that Nostradamus intuited that this was the future the King Henri IV. He sketched out his horoscope. He was lucky enough to show up on the following morning. He was able to look at the moles that were on his body and announce his future as a royal. This was actually amounted to treason. It also signified the end of the dynasty Valois as well. And even though Henri IV was known to tell the story that he actually did succeed to the throne there is no indication that anyone taken note to this point. When the court and its cavalcade was held up at Arles by the flooding waters of the Rhone, Nostradamus was again summoned to attend the royal family, and appointed Councillor and Physician-in-Ordinary to the King. In addition to this position, he was given an income. The seer, who is now the father of six children with his second wife, can be said to have had the success he desired. But, he was severely ill and afflicted by chronic arthritis that made the process almost impossible to take a horse on his back.

The year was 1566. Nostradamus was in the process of dying. His prophecies, that are referred to as the Presages in 1566, a prediction states that 'When he returns to the embassy, he takes away the King's present. The family and friends of his discover him dead in his bench and bed. He was given Extreme Unction in the night of July 1st and confided to his assistant Chavigny who was his assistant, that 'You'll never find me alive until sunrise. It was actually, buried on the floor lying in the manner predicted in the Presages. His body was not even cool. He passed away on July 2 as a day of celebration for those who celebrate the Visitation of Our Lady (Notre Notre Dame) and was laid to rest with full honors at the old Franciscan chapel located in Salon. The tombstone he buried was later replaced by a memorial on the west side in The Chapel of Our Lady - the same place as Notre Dame. His sons had quite well, however the third was killed during a duality and thus was forced to be a friar. His daughter was the one who did not want to get married even though that all the other children were married, only three children were born. Two sons were his daughters. The third daughter of one of his brothers. So the title Nostradamus did not pass on to the next generation.

It may have not mattered for the sage. It's possible that his real, hidden loyalty was to the Goddess and also to old pagan spiritual traditions. The repeated theme of "Our Lady" could suggest this.

Stories of Seer Seer

The stories naturally revolve around people such as Nostradamus and reflect the mystery and charisma of his appearance. Although they may be anecdotes, they do portray Nostradamus in the way we imagine him. The most intriguing stories, which suggests the inevitability of Fate is the choice of the pig that will be burned.

Nostradamus and the Wrong Pig

When visiting a friend for lunch, the hunter saw two piglets in the yard with one being white and the other black. He said that an wolf could eat the white one, and the black one was consumed at dinner. Looking to play a game with his guest, and test whether he can show him wrong, the hosts ordered to have the white piglet be killed to make room for dinner menu, then cooked by his chef. He followed the instructions instructed and the piglet of white was slaughtered and ready for spit roasting and the cook dumped the carcass to the side for a short time. When he left, an obedient wolf-cub keeping on the farm walked to the kitchen, and cooked food out from the porcine carcass. The piglet was not mentioned again or discussed, but the pork was served as a supper dish. The host was joking with Nostradamus informing him that the pig was actually the pig with white skin that they were eating. But the seer insisted that it was actually not the case. For the sake of settling the issue, the cook was called in. He had to acknowledge to the cook that his white pig been killed by a wolf. He also had to admit that it was his responsibility to kill the pig that was black for the dinner, and it was actually the black pig that was still sitting on their plates!

This tale has a delightful twist. It was however not printed until one century following the death of the seer and the story was published unanonymously.

Nostradamus and the Future Pope

When he was on the road in Italy close to Ancona, Nostradamus met a native swineherd (in the case of some, the young friar) traveling along the same route. The seer threw himself to the bottom of the mud before the feet of the shocked young man. He then told him that he had to kneel before His Holiness. In 1585, the boy, Felice Peretti, did actually receive the papal crown and became Sixtus V.